KS3 Science

Essential SATS Practice

It's packed with lots of nasty questions — because they're the sort you'll get in the exam.

They're organised by topic, so you can easily see the types of questions you might get on each area of the curriculum.

Practise getting these questions right and you'll sweat a lot less on the big day.

Contents

Section One — Electricity and Magnetism

Section Two — Forces and Motion

Section Three — Light and Sound

Section Four — The Earth and Beyond

Section Five — Energy Resources and Energy

Published by Coordination Group Publications Ltd.

Contributors:
Stuart Barker, Martin Chester, Kate Manson, Becky May, Barry Pywell, Emma Singleton and James Wallis.

ISBN: 1-84146-241-1

Groovy website: www.cgpbooks.co.uk

With thanks to Ian Francis and Jennifer Underwood for the proofreading.
Jolly bits of clipart from CorelDRAW

Printed by Elanders Hindson, Newcastle upon Tyne

KS3 Physics

Essential SATS Practice

Levels 5-7

CGP

Answers

Contents

Published by Coordination Group Publications Ltd

Groovy website: www.cgpbooks.co.uk

Printed by Elanders Hindson, Newcastle upon Tyne.

Section One — Electricity and Magnetism

Page 1

1 (a) Graphite. **Also accept** 'some solutions', 'carbon'.

(b) (i) An insulator.

(ii) **Any two from** — wood / plastic / rubber / glass / ceramics. **Or any other sensible answer.**

(c) The metal in the core is a conductor and will carry electricity. The plastic in the sheath is an insulator and stops anyone touching the cable from getting an electric shock.

2 (a) B (b) The glass in the rod is an insulator (doesn't conduct electricity). **and** There is a gap in the circuit.

Page 2

1 (a) (i) Electrons. (ii) Negative.

(b) (i) An ammeter. (ii) Amps / Amperes.

2 (a) (i)

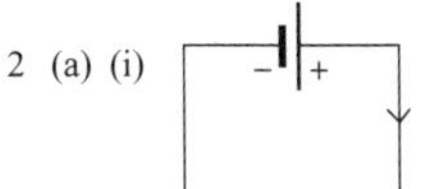

(ii)

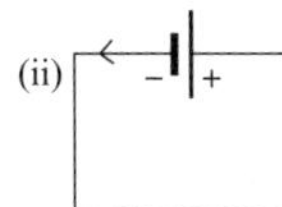

Remember — charge and conventional current always flow in opposite directions.

Arrows can be anywhere, as long as they point the right way.

(b) It would stop flowing.

Page 3

1 (a) The battery is like a pump because it pushes the charge around the circuit.

(b) The wires are like the pipes because they connect the components in the circuit so the charge can flow around it.

(c) The current is like the water because it flows round the circuit and is not used up.

(d) A resistor is like a narrow pipe because it creates resistance to the flow.

2 (a) Bennie. (b) Tamar is not right because charge cannot be used up.

Page 4

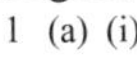

1 (a) (i)

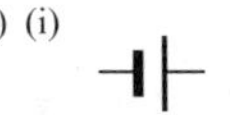

(ii)

(b) (i) Buzzer. (ii) Ammeter.

(c) **1** is a closed switch (on switch), **2** is an open switch (off switch).

2 (a)

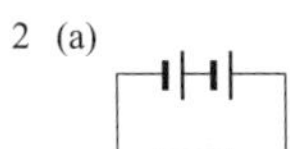

(b)

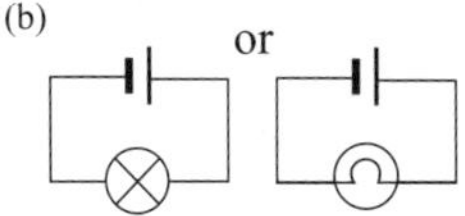

(c)

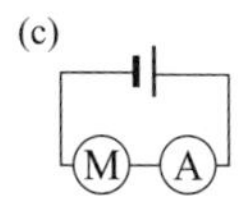

Page 5

1 (a) In a series circuit, the current can only flow through one route. The current is the same in each part of the circuit.

(b)

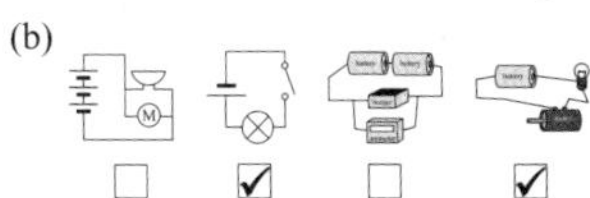

2 (a) More slowly. The buzzer increases the resistance of the circuit.

(b) The current will flow through the wire instead as it gives much less resistance.

Page 6

1 (a) 6.5 A (b) All the lights will go off.

2 (a) (i) 10.0 A. There is half the resistance of circuit 1. The battery will be able to push twice the current.

(ii) 12.0 A. There is twice the push of circuit 1 for the same resistance. There will be twice the current / the voltage has been doubled.

(b)

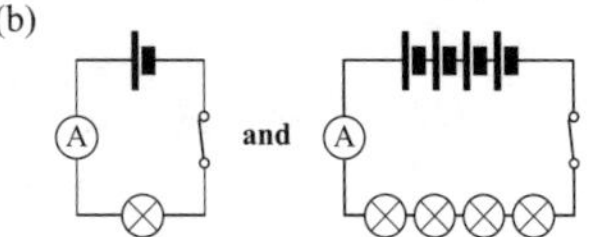

This is series stuff, this. Remember that in series circuits the current can only follow one route.

Page 7

1 (a) A parallel circuit branches. The current can follow more than one route.

(b) (i) A_1 (ii) A_3

(c) (i) A_1, because it shows the total current flowing through the circuit.

(ii) No. Current will differ depending on the components' different resistances.

(iii) A_4. There's no component connected so this branch will have the least resistance to the current.

Page 8

1 (a)

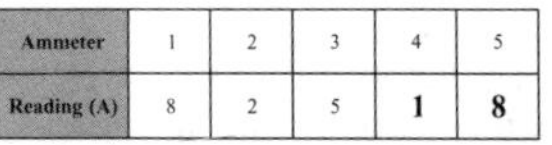

Ammeter	1	2	3	4	5
Reading (A)	8	2	5	**1**	**8**

(b) Ammeter **1** is faulty.

2

Bulbs		
1	2	3
off	on	on
on	**off**	**off**
on	**off**	**on**
on	**on**	**off**
on	**off**	**off**
on	**off**	**off**
on	**on**	**on**

Page 9

1 (a) A magnetic field is a region where a force affects magnetic materials.

(b) (i) It will point from north to south along the field lines.

(ii)

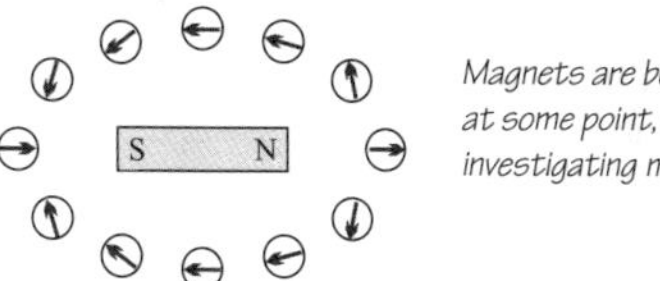

Magnets are bound to come up in the exam at some point, so learn this stuff on investigating magnetic fields really well.

(c) Scatter iron / steel / nickel / cobalt filings around a bar magnet. They will align along the field lines.

(d)

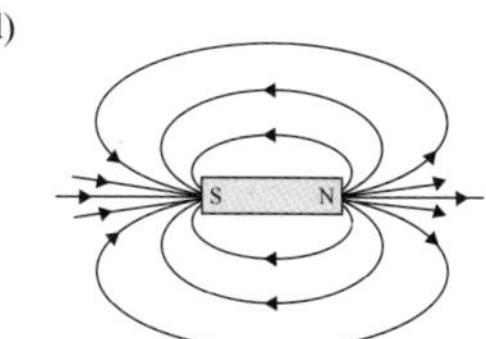

Page 10

1 (a) (i) Copper is not magnetic. (ii) **Any two from** — Steel / nickel / cobalt.

(b) (i) The paperclips might be attracted to the iron because they are magnets.

(ii) Use a known magnet to check if the iron will repel it.

2 (a) [S N] [N S] or [N S] [S N]

(b) [S N] [S N] or [N S] [N S]

Page 11

1 (a) A coil of wire is wrapped around a metal / iron / steel / nickel core and an electric current passed through it.

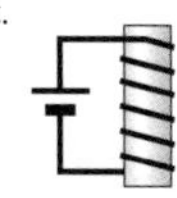

(b) Increase the current. **and** Increase the number of turns of wire around the core. Also accept 'Use soft iron core'.

(c) A steel core would remain magnetised after the current was switched off.

2 (a) Current in the coil turns on electromagnet. This attracts the hammer, which rings the bell whilst breaking the circuit and turning off the electromagnet. The hammer springs back and makes the circuit again. The cycle is then repeated continuously.

(b) A permanent magnet would keep the hammer on the bell. **and** The electromagnet is stronger.

Page 12

1 (a) (i) A relay.

(ii) Using a small current to switch on a larger current in another circuit.

(b) (i) Circuit **B** is an input circuit. Circuit **A** is an output circuit.

(ii) The input of pressing the switch gives the output of the hand drier turning on.

(c) Current in the coil turns on the electromagnet, attracting the iron lever. It pivots and pushes the contacts together, turning on the heater and fan.

(d) There is a risk of electric shock, especially if the drier is switched on with wet hands. A shock from mains electricity would be more dangerous than a shock from the input circuit.

Page 13

1 (a) (i) The movement of charge / electrons around a circuit. (ii) Conductors.

(b)

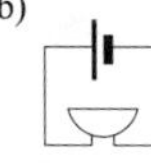

(c) In series. If she connects them in parallel, the buzzer will work regardless of whether the material is a conductor.

(d) (i) **Any three metals, e.g.** copper, iron, brass, **also graphite / carbon. Accept:** 'Some solutions'.

(ii) **Any three from** — wood, plastic, rubber, glass, ceramics. **Or any other sensible answer.**

Page 14

2 (a) (i) A coil of wire. (ii) An electromagnet.

(b) (i)

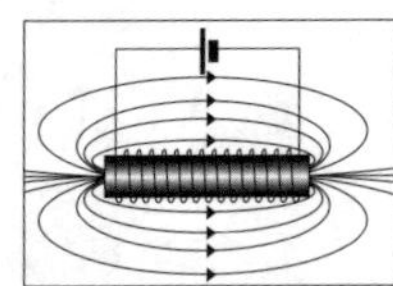

(ii) It will be reversed. / The north pole becomes the south pole.

(c) Add more batteries (cells). / Increase the current. **and** Increase the number of turns on the solenoid. **and** Use a soft iron core for the electromagnet.

Page 15

2 (d) (i) **Any two from** — iron, nickel, cobalt, steel.

(ii) These are magnetic. Non-magnetic materials won't be attracted to a magnet.

(e) B, C (f) A

(g) (i) C. With the switch closed, current will flow through the wire around the electromagnet because of its much lower resistance.

(ii) A short circuit.

Page 16

3 (a)

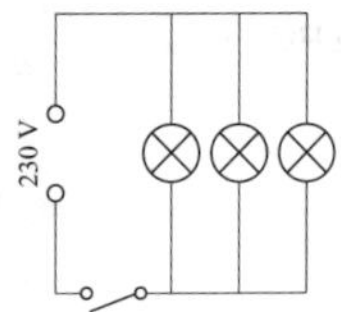

(b) In series. If it was connected in parallel, current would still be able to flow through the rest of the circuit.

4 (a) A_2 **3 A** A_3 **3 A** A_4 **3 A** A_5 **3 A** A_6 **12 A**

(b) No, A_1 and A_6 have the same ammeter reading.

(c) The current. **Accept** The battery.

Section Two — Forces and Motion

Page 17

1 (a) t = 60 s = 1 minute = 1/60 hours
s = d/t = 1 / 1/60 = 60 miles/hour

(b) (i) t = d/s = 1/200 hours **or** 0.005 hours

(ii) t = 1/200 × 60 × 60 s = 18 s

(c) t = 3 minutes = 3/60 hours = 0.05 hours
d = s × t = 120 × 0.05 = 6 miles

If you learn your formula triangles really well then questions like this will be a doddle in the exam.

2 (a) s = d/t = 700m / 10mins = 70m/min
(multiply both by 60 to find answer per hour)
s = 4200m/hour (divide metres by 1000 to get answer in km)
Jenny's speed = 4.2km/hour

(b) t = d/s = 0.5km / 4km/hr
t = 0.125 hours (multiply by 60 to get time in mins)
t = 7.5 mins, so Chris took less time than Jenny to reach the beach.

Page 18

1 (a) Through liquid B.

(b) d = 50 cm = 50/100 m = 0.5 m
s = d/t = 0.5/5 = 0.1 m/s

(c) t = d/s = 0.5/1.0 = 0.5 s

(d) t = d/s = 15/2.5 = 6 s

(e) d = s × t = 0.4 × 23 = 9.2 m

Page 19

1 (a) 76 minutes. (b) 4 minutes.

(c) (i) 10 miles/hour.

(ii) t = 39 - 30 = 9 minutes = 9/60 hours = 0.15 hours
d = s × t = 10 × 0.15 = 1.5 miles

(d) t = 6 minutes = 6/60 hours = 0.1 hours
s = d/t = 4.4/0.1 = 44 miles/hour

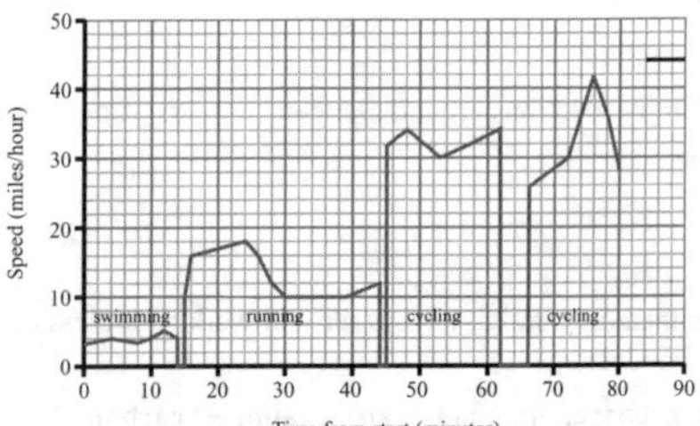

Don't be put off by graph-based questions like this. They only test you on familiar things (like speed calculations in this case) — it's just the information is displayed in a different way.

(e) t = 45 minutes = 45/60 hours = 0.75 hours
s = d/t = 24/0.75 = 32 miles/hour

Page 20

1 (a) (i) A newton meter / forcemeter. (ii) Newtons.

(b) (i) Gravity (**Accept** 'Weight'). (ii) The spring / newton meter / hook.

(c) They are equal / balanced.

2 (a) The strawberry will stay where it is. (b) The strawberry will sink into the cream.

Page 21

1 (a) Speed up. (b) Slow down. (c) Change direction.

2 (a) (i) C (ii) B (iii) A

(b) A. It shows the mass at rest, after it has stopped bouncing on the rope.

(c) It changes shape / stretches.

Page 22

1 (a) A frictional force which acts against objects moving through air.

(b) (i) There's no air resistance in a vertical sense / direction, because the skydiver isn't moving through the air.

(ii) It increases as his speed increases.

(c) (i) It increases a lot.

(ii) Air resistance and weight become equal / balanced.
No overall force acts on the skydiver and he falls at a steady speed.

(d)

	Diagram	Label
1	Z	C
2	V	E
3	Y	B
4	X	A
5	W	D

Air resistance and friction are both types of force.

Page 23

1 (a) **Any two from** — It makes the tyres grip the road surface. / It allows the brakes to grip the wheels. / It holds together parts fixed by screws, nuts and bolts, etc. / It allows the rider to grip the bike. **Or any other sensible answer.**

(b) **Any two from** — Energy is lost due to friction between moving parts. / Energy is lost in overcoming air resistance. / Air resistance limits the top speed of the bike. **Or any other sensible answer.**

(c) A. It is more streamlined / aerodynamic so less affected by air resistance.

(d) B. It is less streamlined / aerodynamic so causes more air resistance and needs more energy to overcome it.

Page 24

1 (a)

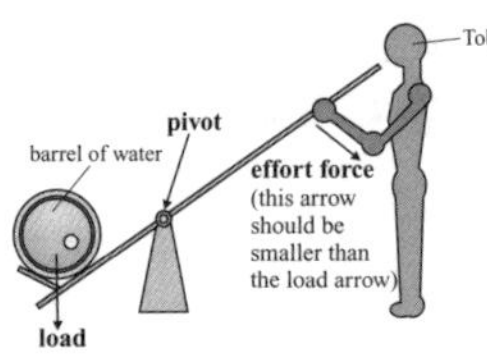

This stuff on pivots and loads might seem complicated at first, but once you've got your head round the basic principles, you'll start seeing examples all over the place, and it'll all make sense.

(b) The point that a lever rotates around.

(c) A lever can be called a machine because it can make a job easier.
In the diagram, the force needed to lift the barrel is not as large as the weight of the barrel, because the lever multiplies the effort force.

(d) (i) Grip the lever further from the pivot.

(ii) The longer the lever, the smaller the effort force needed to move a load.

Page 25

1 (a)

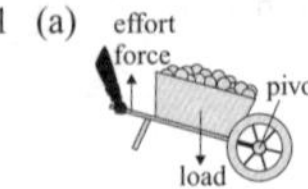

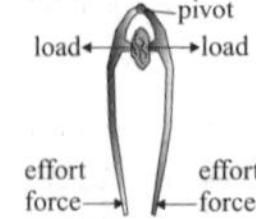

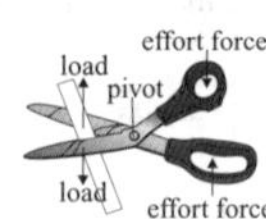

(b) (i) A

(ii) The distance from the effort force to the pivot will be longer. **and** The distance from the pivot to the load is shorter.

2 (a)

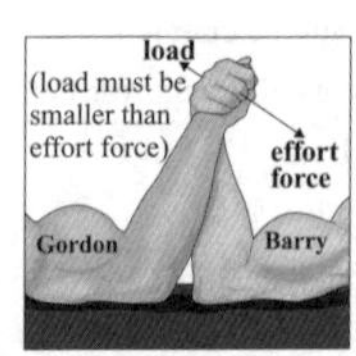

Phwoar, look at the muscles on those boys. Remember that arms are an exception to the rule — the effort from the muscles must always be greater than the load.

(b) The effort force must be greater than the load. / The distance from the pivot to the effort force is less than the distance from the pivot to the load.

Page 26

1 (a) (i) Moment. (ii) Nm / Ncm

(b) $M = F \times r = 10\ N \times 0.25\ m = 2.5\ Nm$

(c) $M = F \times r$
$2.5 = 4 \times r$
$r = 2.5 / 4 = 0.625$ m **or** 62.5 cm

(d) Anticlockwise: $M = F \times r = 4 \times 0.1 = 0.4$ Nm
Clockwise: $M = F \times r$
$0.4 = F \times 0.25$
$F = 0.4/0.25 = 1.6$ N

It only takes a moment to learn how to calculate a moment — then questions like these will soon be a breeze.

Page 27

1 (a) $M = F \times r = 4000 \times 2/100 = 80$ Nm

Don't forget to change the cm into m to get the right units.

(b) (i) Smaller. The weight will create a moment that is equal and opposite to the moment created by the muscles. It is further from the pivot, so the weight will be smaller than the force exerted by the muscles.

(ii) $F = M/r = 80 / 40/100 = 80/0.4 = 200$ N **or**
$M = F \times r$
$80 = F \times 40/100 = F \times 0.4$
$F = 80/0.4 = 200$ N

(iii) His arm will straighten. **or** He will not be able to keep his elbow bent. **or** The forearm will move clockwise. **or** He will not be able to hold it steady.

Page 28

1 (a) (i) $M = F \times r = 1025\ N \times 0.1\ m = 102.5$ Nm

(ii) $M = F \times r = (1025\ N \times 0.1\ m) + (1025\ N \times 0.1\ m) = 205$ Nm **or**
$M = 2 \times 102.5\ Nm = 205$ Nm

(b) (i) Moment for 1 rocket = 102.5 Nm
Number of rockets needed = 820/102.5 = 8 rockets

(ii) Increase the distance of the rockets from the pivot.

Page 29

1 (a) (i) $P = F/A = 12/0.1 = 120\ N/cm^2$

(ii) $120\ N/cm^2 = 120 \times 10\,000\ N/m^2 = 1\,200\,000\ N/m^2$

(iii) $1\,200\,000\ N/m^2 = 1\,200\,000$ Pa

(b) The same force is spread out over a larger area, so the pressure on the wall is lower.

2 (a) $2 \times 12\,000$ Pa = 24 000 Pa. The area that Max's weight acts over is halved, so the pressure on the floor doubles.

(b) $F = P \times A = 12\,000 \times 0.06 = 720$ N

Page 30

1 (a) For A: $P = F/A = 27/(3 \times 20) = 27/60 = 0.45\ N/cm^2$ **or**
$P = F/A = 27 \times 4/(3 \times 20) \times 4 = 108/240 = 0.45\ N/cm^2$
For B: $P = F/A = 27 \times 4/27 \times 20 = 108/540 = 0.2\ N/cm^2$
B puts least pressure on the bookshelf.

(b) It won't.

2 (a) $F = P \times A = 4 \times 9 = 36$ N (b) $A = F/P = 28/4 = 7\ cm^2$

Page 31

1 (a) $P = F/A = 450/0.06 = 7500$ Pa N / m^2. Anne is correct.

(b) It will spread the force over a larger area.

(c) Maximum $F = P \times A = 4000 \times 0.16 = 640$ N
Maximum weight of base = maximum F – weight of statue
= 640 – 450 N = 190 N

2 (a) $P = F/A = 240\,000/8 = 30\,000$ Pa N / m^2

(b) $A = F/P = 240\,000/32\,000 = 7.5\ m^2$
Difference in area = $8 - 7.5\ m^2 = 0.5\ m^2$
He could have made the foundations $0.5\ m^2$ smaller.

Page 32

1 (a) (i) Friction.

(ii) **Any one from** — It makes the tyres grip the road surface. / It allows the brakes to grip the wheels. / It holds together parts fixed by screws, nuts and bolts, etc. / It allows the rider to grip the bike. **Or any other sensible answer.**

(b) It is more streamlined / aerodynamic / causes less air resistance / drag.

(c) $s = d/t = 0.15 \times 1000/12.5 = 12$ m/s **or** $s = d/t = 0.15/12.5 = 0.012$ km/s
or $s = d/t = 0.15/(12.5/60/60) = 43.2$ km/h to 3 s.f.

(d) (i) 120 N. The bicycle is travelling at a constant speed, so the forces acting on it are balanced.

(ii) The backward force is greater than the forward force and the bicycle slows down. As it slows, the backward force decreases and becomes equal to the forward force. The bicycle then travels at a constant speed.

Page 33

2 (a) (i) $P = F/A = 50/2 = 25\ N/cm^2$ (ii) $F = P \times A = 25 \times 25 = 625$ N

(b) (i) $M = F \times r = 450 \times 0.14 = 63$ Nm (ii) $F = M/r = 35/0.14 = 250$ N

Page 34

3 (a) (i)

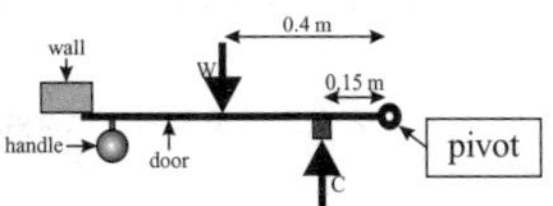

(ii) Force W is the **load**. Force C is the **effort force**.

(b) (i) $F = P \times a = 20 \times 1.6 = 32$ N (ii) $M = F \times r = 32 \times 0.4 = 12.8$ Nm

(iii) Yes. The anticlockwise moment produced by the wind is greater than the clockwise moment produced by the closing device so the door will move anticlockwise.

Page 35

3 (c) $M = F \times r = 10 \times 0.15 = 1.5$ Nm

(d) (i) 1.5 Nm. Jessica is holding the door still, so the 2 opposing moments are equal.

(ii) $F = M/r = 1.5/0.75 = 2$ N

(e) When the door isn't moving, the moments produced by forces J and C about the pivot are equal. Because force J is exerted further from the pivot than force C, it is smaller than force C.

(f) (i) The door will open further. (ii) The door will close further.

(g) Increase the force applied by the device to the door. **and** Increase the perpendicular distance of the device from the pivot.

Section Three — Light and Sound

Page 36

1 (a) (i) [and (b) (i)]

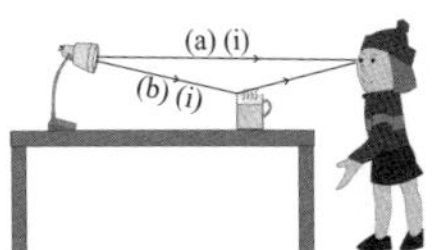

Remember that light always travels in straight lines — so you should use a ruler to draw straight light rays in your answers, so you don't lose easy marks.

(ii) The light bulb is luminous / a light source so light travels in a straight line from the bulb to Charmaine's eye.

(iii) **Any two luminous objects, e.g.** the Sun, a star, a candle, a flame.

(b) (i) See diagram above.

(ii) **Any two non-luminous objects, e.g.** the Moon, a book, a person.

(iii) The mug is non-luminous / not a light source. Light from elsewhere must reflect off the mug before Charmaine can see it.

Page 37

1 (a) tracing paper screen

(b) The pinhole lets in very few rays. Because they travel in straight lines the rays must cross over, reversing the image.

2 (a) (i) The fireworks are luminous / produce light.

(ii) The fireworks would be paler, other light sources would blot them out.

(b) (i) Arif. The sound takes longer to travel to him.

(ii) Light is faster than sound, because it reaches them both first. It must also be a lot faster than sound, since it reaches them at the same time even though they are different distances away.

Page 38

1 (a) (b)

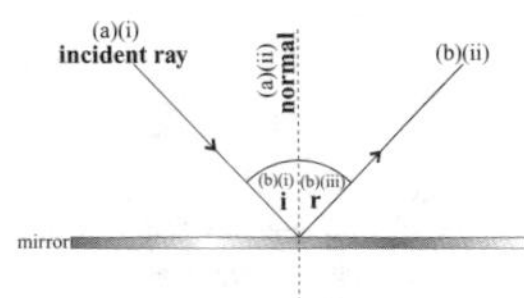

(c) (i) The angle of incidence is equal to the angle of reflection. **or** i = r

(ii) The mirror has a smooth, shiny surface that reflects all incident rays at the same angle.

(iii) Light falls on an object that has a rough / non-smooth surface.

Page 39

1 (a) It travels in straight lines.

(b)

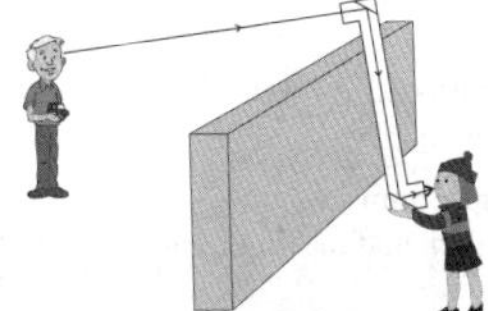

The ray of light has reflected off Johan, and should be pointing towards Claire's eyes, as this is how she sees him.

2 (a) (i) It passes through the glass (is transmitted).

(ii) It has a smooth, shiny surface that reflects all incident rays at the same angle.

(b) (i) Diffuse (reflection).

(ii) The rough surface causes incident rays to be reflected back at varying angles.

Page 40

1 (a)

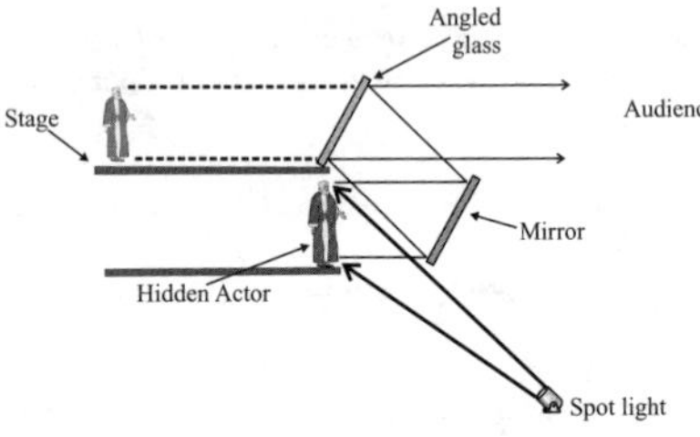

Bit of a tricky question, this. The principles are the same — you just have to use your noddle a bit and apply them to a new situation.

(b) By switching off the light that shines on the hidden actor.

(c) The audience is able to see both the ghost and the actors on stage. The glass both reflects light and allows light to pass through it.

(d) **Any three uses of mirrors, e.g.** a make-up mirror, a shaving mirror, a car rear-view mirror, as a reflector in a lamp, in a kaleidoscope, in a periscope, in a telescope.

Page 41

1 (a) (i) They are all transparent. (ii) Refraction.

(b) The speed of light depends on the density of the medium it is in. When it passes from one medium to another, the change in density means that its speed will change and it will bend.

(c)

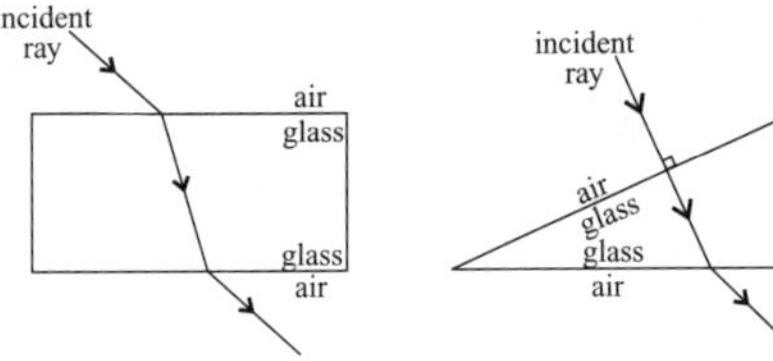

Page 42

1 (a) The angle of the incident ray to the normal.

(b) Water. In the experiments, light is bent because it slows down. It bends less when it enters water than it does when it enters glass, so it can't have slowed as much.

(c) **The refracted ray should show that the light has bent towards the normal but only by a little, e.g.**

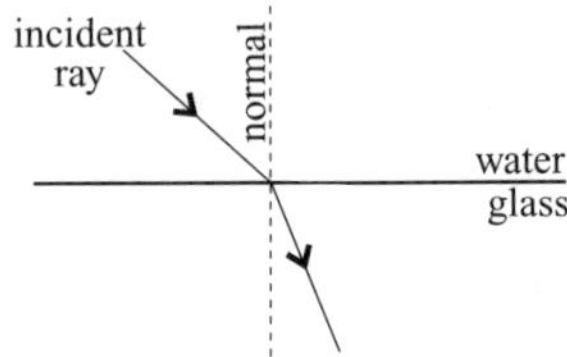

Refraction can be hard to get your head round — but as long as you learn the rules about how light bends towards or away from the normal depending on the density of the media, then you'll be fine.

Page 43

1 (a) It's opaque.

(b)

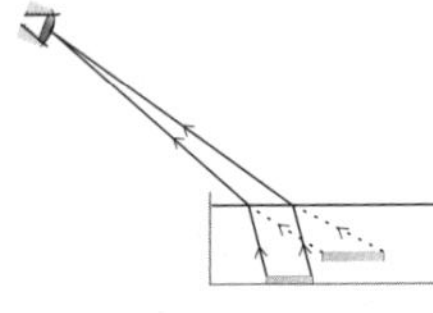

These kinds of questions about refraction in water are common in the exam — so get down the swimming pool and start learning...

(c) Before (i.e. nearer to himself).

(d) Light travelling from under the water is refracted at the surface. The pool looks as it would if the light was travelling in a straight line, which makes the bottom look closer than it is.

Page 44

1 (a) (i) Spectrum. (ii) Dispersal.

(b) (i) Red. (ii) Violet.

(iii) The light bends as it enters and leaves the prism. The different colours bend by different amounts.

(c) Sunlight is a mixture of all the colours in the spectrum. Rain drops refract sunlight, dispersing the sunlight and making a rainbow.

Page 45

1 (a) A Colour = **Red**, Explanation: **The flower reflects only red light, which passes through the filter.**

B Colour = **Red**, Explanation: **The flower reflects the red light, which passes through the filter.**

C Colour = **Black**, Explanation: **There is no red light for the flower to reflect, so it looks black.**

D Colour = **Black**, Explanation: **The flower reflects red light, which passes through magenta filter but is absorbed by the blue filter.**

(b) Black. The leaves will reflect only green light. There is green light only in A, but this will be absorbed by the filter.

Page 46

1 (a) Light can travel through a vacuum but sound cannot, and space is a vacuum.

(b) Touching helmets means that the sound always has a medium to travel through. The vibrations pass from the air in Zak's helmet, to the touching helmets, to the air in Joel's helmet, to Joel's ear.

2 (a) (i) An echo. (ii) It was reflected from the walls of the cave.

(b) The vibrations take time to travel to the cave walls and back again.

(c) The sound has lost/less energy.

(d) Measure the time between the clap and its echo. Use half this time and the speed of sound to calculate the distance to the wall the sound is reflected from.

Page 47

1 (a) The height of the wave (measured from the mid point). (b) They are equally loud.

(c) **Any two from** — Ivan played the note more quietly. / Ivan was further from the microphone when he played the note. / Ivan changed the settings of the oscilloscope.

2 (a) (i) The rock band. The wave has the largest amplitude.

(ii) The sound had most energy.

(b) **The trace should look similar to the trace for quiet talking, but with a smaller amplitude, e.g.**

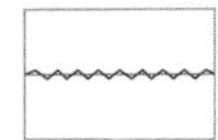

Page 48

1 (a) (i) The number of waves that pass a point in one second. **or** The number of waves made per second.

(ii) The higher the frequency, the higher a noise's pitch.

(b) 1 A road drill, 2 A car engine, 3 A dentist's drill, 4 A scream.

2 (a) B. It contains waves with three different frequencies. (b) A

(c)

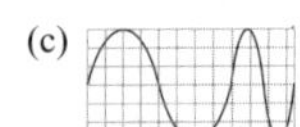

Page 49

1 (a)

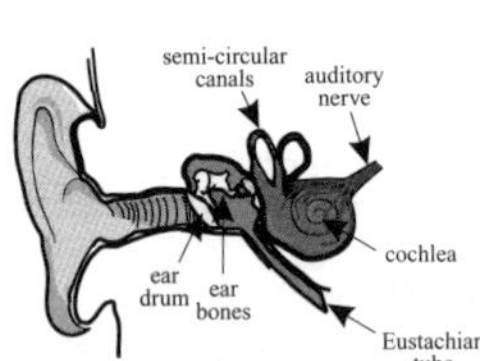

This might seem more like biology than physics, but you need to know the structure of the ear for the exam, so no complaining.

(b) The vibrations are passed from Julie's vocal chords to the air, to Heather's ear drum, then to her ear bones and on to her cochlea. Hairs in her cochlea vibrate, triggering the nerve cells of the auditory nerve. The signals are sent to Heather's brain, which turns them into the sound of Julie's whisper.

(c) (i) Decibels (ii) **Any estimate in the range** 1–20.

(iii) The teacher is older than Julie. Younger people hear quiet sounds better.

Page 50

1 (a) Gradually increase the frequency of the sounds. The highest frequency that the person still raises their hand at is the maximum value in the range. Then gradually decrease the frequency of the sounds to find the minimum.

(b) **Any two from** — They should be the same distance from the loudspeaker. / The loudspeaker should be set at the same volume. / The increases or decreases in frequency should be the same size. / They should have the same number of attempts at hearing a frequency. **Or any other sensible answer.**

(c)

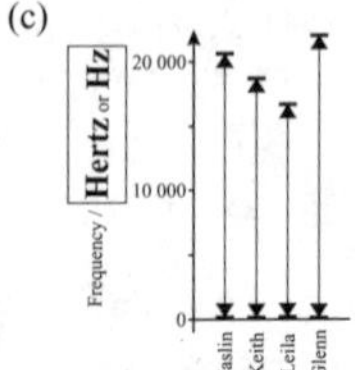

(d) (i) Glenn (ii) Leila (iii) Glenn

(e) **Any two from** — Ears are blocked, for example with wax. / Nerve damage. / Damage caused by illness or infection.

Page 51

1 (a)

	60 dB	80 dB
8000 Hz	D	A
10 000 Hz	B	C

(b) D and B, A and C

2 (a) Light travels so quickly that it reached William Derham at virtually the same time the cannon was fired.

(b) (i) The sound travelled by making the air particles vibrate. Wind also moves the air particles and could interfere with the sound vibrations.

(ii) He averaged several results.

Page 52

3 (a) It is transparent.

(b) (i) It will bend / be refracted.

(ii) Glass is more dense than air, and light travels more slowly through it. The change in speed causes the light to bend as it enters the glass.

(iii)

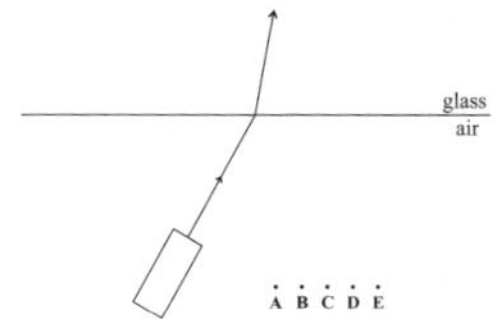

(c) D. For reflected light, angle of reflection = angle of incidence.

Page 53

3 (d) (i) All of the light will be reflected at the same angle.

(ii) Nearly all of the light will be reflected, but at different angles.

(e) (i) A green spot. The green screen reflects green light. Accept 'nothing'.

(ii) No spot. The red screen absorbs all colours of light except red.

(f) (i) A spectrum. White light is a mixture of colours, and is dispersed by a prism.

(ii) A blue spot. The filter absorbs all colours of light except blue.

Page 54

4 (a) (i) The sea bed. (ii) The pulse that comes back after 1 s indicates an object in the sea, which may be a shoal of fish.

(b) (i) B (ii) C (iii) A

(c) The sound's energy becomes more and more spread out, so the amplitude of the wave decreases.

(d) The sound is outside the audible range of pitch of humans, but not of dolphins.

Section Four — The Earth and Beyond

Page 55

1 (a) Day time changes to night time as the Earth rotates on its axis and turns away from the light from the Sun.

(b) It is midday. **B**, The Sun has just set. **KL**

2 (a) 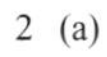

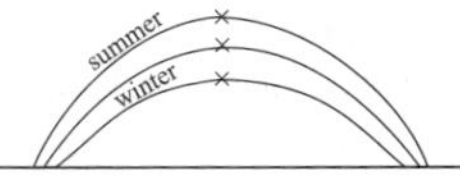

This is an easy question — the Sun is always higher in the sky in summer and lower in winter.

(b) During winter. The Sun is lowest in the sky at midday.

(c) It appears to move from east to west.

Page 56

1 (a) (i) The time it takes the Earth to orbit once around the sun.

(ii) It takes 365¼ days for the Earth to orbit the sun. We say a year is 365 days, so a year with an 'extra' day is needed every fourth year.

(b) (i) B (ii) A

(c) The time spent in sunlight. / The length of the days. **and** The area sunlight is spread over.

(d) At the same time as the northern hemisphere is tilted away from the Sun, the southern hemisphere is tilted towards it.

Page 57

1 (a) Moons are natural objects which orbit planets.

(b) It reflects light from the Sun. It's bright because it's so close to the Earth.

(c) From the Earth, different amounts of the sunlit part of the Moon are visible at different points during its orbit.

(d) (i) C (ii) B, D (iii) F, H (iv) G

Page 58

1 (a) (i) Gravity

(ii)

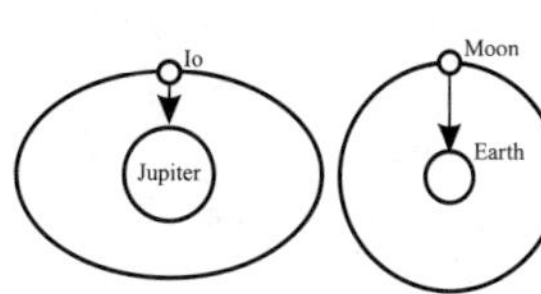

Be careful with this question — even though the moon and planet attract each other by gravity, the force that keeps the moon in orbit round the planet should point from the moon to the planet.

(b) It will be larger. The larger the mass, the stronger the force of gravity.

(c) Other moons exert gravitational forces on Io that change its movement.

2 (a) It decreased. The mass of the satellite decreased, and the force of gravity depends on the mass involved.

(b) It will increase. The closer objects are, the stronger their gravitational attraction.

Page 59

1 (a) The signals travel in straight lines, so would be blocked by Earth's curved surface.

(b) (i) It completes an orbit in the same time as the Earth completes a rotation.

(ii) 24 hours / 1 day.

(c) **Any three from** — Navigation, weather monitoring / forecasting, spying, mapping, observing the Earth, observing / exploring space. **Or any other sensible answer.**

Page 60

1 (a) An object that orbits around a star. (b) They reflect light from the Sun.

(c) It is the closest planet to Earth. **Accept** Clouds in its atmosphere reflect sunlight.

(d) It is obscured by light from the Sun.

2 (a)

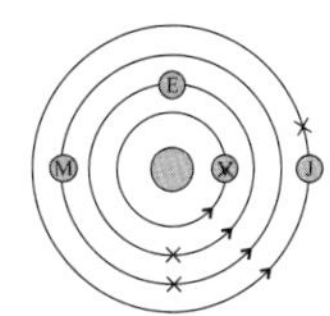

Simple maths should do the trick here — all the information you need is in the table.

(b) The further a planet is from the Sun, the longer its orbit time.

(c) They are circular instead of elliptical. They are not to scale / do not show the relative distances travelled. **Or any other sensible answer.**

Page 61

1 (a) In comparison to the Earth. / **Accept** 'In comparison to each other.'

(b) (i) Jupiter. (ii) Pluto. (iii) Venus.

(c) (i) Uranus. (ii) Neptune.

(iii) The size of a planet is its volume / dimensions / diameter. The mass of a planet is how much matter it contains.

(d) It is not a planet, it is a star.

(e) **Any two from** — asteroids / planetoids / minor planets / moons / satellites / comets / meteors / meteorites. **Or any other sensible answer.**

Page 62

1 (a) planet Earth, the Sun, Solar System, galaxy, Universe.

(b) (i) A collection of many stars. (ii) The Milky Way. (iii) A small, blurred star.

(c) They are very distant. **and** They are difficult to see in the light from the nearby star. **Or any other sensible answer.**

Page 63

1 (a) The rotation of the Earth.

(b) (i) The Pole Star. **Accept** Polaris. (ii) It is directly above the Earth's axis.

2 (a) B. It has a larger orbit, so is likely to take most time to complete an orbit.

(b) Satellite **A** is likely to be the weather satellite because **as it orbits and the Earth rotates, it will cover the whole surface of the Earth**. Also shorter orbit — more up to date information on changing weather.

Satellite **B** is likely to be the television satellite because **it orbits above the same point on the Earth's surface so will be able to send signals over a fixed area**.

Page 64

3 (a) 365¼ days.

(b) (i) A star. (ii) Its gravity keeps the Earth in orbit. **and** It provides the energy for life. **Or any other sensible answer.**

(c) (i) The Earth rotates once every 24 hours. (ii) A.

Page 65

3 (c) (iii) Because the Earth is tilted on its axis, when it is at A the light from the Sun will reach the same place at more of an angle, making the Sun appear lower in the sky.

0604 - 1669

(iv) The seasons. Because the Earth's axis is tilted, the length of day and the amount of sunlight a place will get depends on the Earth's position in its orbit.

(d) In summer, the Sun is between the Earth and Orion and will swamp the light from the constellation. In winter, it is on the other side of the Earth, leaving the dark side of the Earth facing Orion.

(e) A galaxy. It appears blurred because contains many stars, not just one.

Page 66

4 (a) A force of attraction between objects that have mass.

(b) Because it has the greatest mass, the Sun exerts the greatest force of gravity of any object in the Solar System.

(c) (i) Elliptical / an ellipse.

(ii) The comet has a smaller mass than any of the planets, so it is less strongly attracted to the Sun.

(iii) It will increase. The smaller the distance between objects, the stronger their gravitational attraction between them.

(d) (i) Venus, Mars. (ii) Venus is too hot/close to Sun. Mars is too cold/far from Sun.

Section Five — Energy Resources and Energy

Page 67

1 (a) (i) Kinetic (ii) Chemical (iii) Gravitational (potential) (iv) Light

(b)

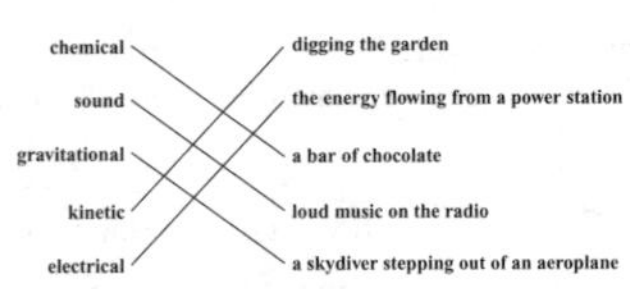

2 (a) No. Any object with a temperature above absolute zero has heat energy. This means that all objects have some heat energy.

(b) No. Heat energy is flowing into his body. Temperature is the measure of that energy.

Page 68

1 (a) 'Electrical to chemical' should be ticked.

(b) 'Chemical to electrical to kinetic' should be ticked.

2 (a) Gravitational (potential) to kinetic.

(b) Electrical to light and sound. **(Accept** heat / thermal).

(c) Chemical to kinetic and sound. **(Accept** heat / thermal).

(d) Electrical to kinetic, heat / thermal and sound.

Don't forget that energy can be converted into more than one form.

Page 69

1 (a) There is a temperature difference between the ends. (b) Conduction.

(c) Particles gaining heat energy at one end of the wire vibrate faster. Some of the energy of vibration is transferred to neighbouring particles, causing them to vibrate, and the energy spreads down the wire.

2 (a) Convection.

(b) Because convection needs particles and vacuums contain no particles.

3 (a) The Sun radiates heat, which is absorbed by the milk tankers.

(b) The shiny silver colour reflects (heat) radiation away from the tanker.

Page 70

1 (a) Photosythesis in plants converts light into chemical energy, which is a more useable form of energy.

(b) Plants (or animals that have eaten plants) die and decay. Over millions of years, they form coal, oil or natural gas, which act as stores of their chemical energy.

(c) Wood **and** food. **Or any other sensible answer.**

(d) Light energy from the Sun is converted into chemical energy by plants, which is converted into heat and kinetic energy when we eat the plants (or animals that have eaten the plants) as food. **or** Light energy from the Sun is converted into chemical energy by trees, which is converted into heat energy when we burn their wood as fuel. **Or any other sensible answer.**

2 (a) (i) Kinetic.

(ii) Heat radiates from the Sun, warming the land, which warms the air above it. This sets up convection currents with cooler air over the sea, and this movement of air creates winds.

(b) Wave power.

Page 71

1 (a) Coal, oil, natural gas. (b) Petrol is too expensive.

(c) **Any two sensible answers, e.g.** lighting, heating, cooking.

2 (a) 1 Letter **B** Name **Boiler**
2 Letter **C** Name **Turbine**
3 Letter **A** Name **Generator**

(b) Fuel is burnt in the boiler, converting chemical energy into heat energy. This is used to heat water, producing steam at high pressure which drives the turbine. The energy has become kinetic. The turbine turns the generator to make electricity, which is fed to the national grid and on to our homes.

Page 72

1 (a) Fossil fuels are used more quickly than they can be replaced. Burning less will mean they will last longer, or can be saved for other important uses. For example, crude oil makes plastics and medicines.

(b) **Any two sensible ways of saving energy, e.g.** turning off lights, using energy-saving light bulbs, driving cars with lower fuel use**.**

(c) (i) **Any three from** — solar power, wind power, wave power, tidal power, hydroelectric power, geothermal power, biomass. **Or any sensible answer.**

(ii) **Accept explanation or example, e.g.** The resources are not re-usable — once transformed, the energy cannot be used again. But resources are renewed — the energy is in continuous supply. **or** Once light from the Sun becomes electrical energy in a solar cell, that light cannot be used again, but more light energy can be gained when the Sun shines again.

2 (a) Solar / light to electrical.

(b) **Any two from** — no batteries to run out, no batteries to throw away, reduces use of non-renewable energy, cheaper**. Or any other sensible answer.**

(c) The calculator will not work without light unless it has a battery as well.

Page 73

1 (a) No. Energy can't be created. It can only be converted from one form to another.

(b) **The following statements should be ticked** — Energy is only useful when it's converted from one form into another. Machines convert input energy into useful output energy.

(c) Machines like computers waste energy in the form of heat and sound, making a room containing computers warmer and noisier than a room without such machines.

2 (a) Input = **electrical** Output = **light** Waste = **heat**

(b) Input = **electrical** Output = **heat, kinetic** Waste = **sound**

Page 74

1 (a) The energy saver light bulb wastes less energy.

(b) **Any two from** — cheaper, uses less energy / saves energy, reduces use of fossil fuels, reduces pollution from electricity generation / they last longer. **Or any other sensible answer.**

2 (a) (i) 25. (ii) 200. (iii) 320.

(b) (i) Kinetic. (ii) Electrical.

(c) (i) The wind turbine. (ii) The lawnmower.

(d) Heat / thermal **and** sound.

Page 75

1 (a) The particles in steel vibrate faster as heat is gained. The energy of vibration passes easily to other particles, spreading the energy quickly.

(b) It prevents heat loss through conduction.

(c) It reflects radiated heat back into the oven to prevent heat loss.

2 (a) Electrical to heat / thermal energy.

(b) (i) All objects with a temperature above absolute zero have heat energy.

(ii) The element has a higher temperature / more heat energy than the water.

(c) (i) Convection.

(ii) The water particles around the element rise as they gain energy. The element is at the bottom so that there is room for this. A convection current is set up that replaces the hot water with cold, so that all the water in the kettle is heated.

Page 76

3 (a) (i) Energy can never disappear, only be converted from one form to another.

(ii) **Missing words: 40** J of useful **kinetic** energy out. 60 J of wasted **heat** energy and **sound** energy. (**These can be in either order.**)

Page 77

3 (b) **Missing words in this order** — gravitational potential, kinetic, kinetic, electrical

(c) (i) Photosynthesis in plants converts light from the Sun into chemical energy. This is stored in the remains of dead plants (or animals that ate the plants), which over millions of years form coal.

(ii) It heats the world, providing energy to evaporate water which will later fall as rain.

(d) (i) **Any one from** — thermal / heat, sound.

(ii) Coal is a fossil fuel, which unlike hydroelectric energy is non-renewable and will run out.

Page 78

4 (a) (i) Chemical. (ii) In John's muscles.

(b) (i) Gravitational potential **and** kinetic. (ii) Gravitational potential.

(c) (i) Gravitational potential to kinetic energy.

(ii) Kinetic to thermal / heat **or** sound energy **(accept either).**

Phew, the last question in the book. Give yourself a well-earned break and go and listen to some music or watch TV (whilst noting the energy transformations taking place...).

Electrical Conductors

1 A material that allows electricity to flow through it is called a **conductor**.
Metals are conductors.

(a) Name **one** non-metal that is also a conductor.

....

(b) (i) What name is given to a material that does **not** allow charge to pass through it?

....

(ii) Give **two** examples of materials that do not allow charge to pass through them.

1 .... 2 ....

(c) Explain why electrical cables are usually made with a metal core surrounded by a plastic cover.

....

....

....

2 Two electrical circuits are shown below.

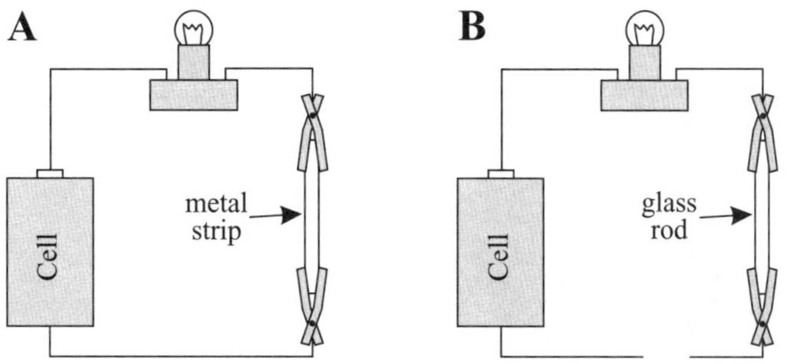

A

Cell

metal strip

B

Cell

glass rod

(a) In which circuit will the bulb **not** light, A or B? ....

(b) Give **two** reasons for your answer to (a).

1 ....

2 ....

Electric Current

1 An electric current is the movement of charge around a circuit.

(a) (i) What are the moving charges that make up an electric current?

....

(ii) Are these charges positive or negative?

....

(b) (i) What instrument is used to measure electric current?

....

(ii) What units are used to measure electric current?

....

2 Both of the circuits below have current flowing through them.

(a) Draw **one** arrow on each diagram to show which direction:

(i) **conventional current** flows around a circuit.

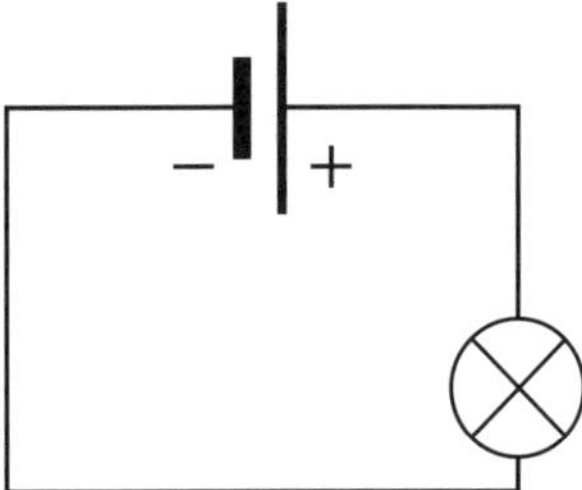

(ii) **charge** flows around a circuit.

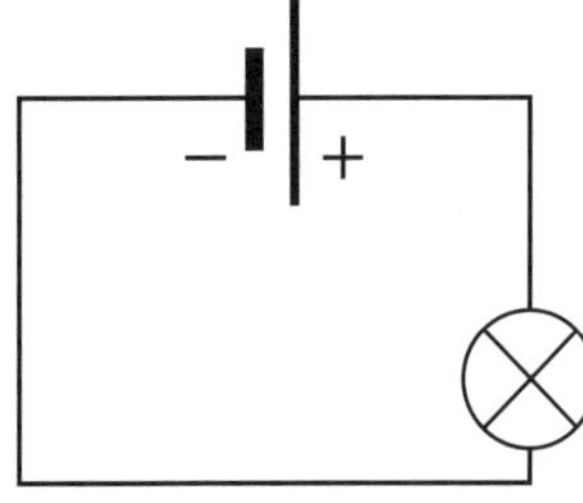

(b) What would happen to the current if there was a break in the circuit?

....

Electric Current

1 An electrical circuit can be compared to a system of water pipes. Choose from the list below to give the electrical equivalent for each part of a water system, and explain why they are similar.

wires charge current switch flow battery bulb resistor

(a) **The** .... **is like a pump because** ....

....

(b) **The** .... **are like the pipes because** ....

....

(c) **The** .... **is like the water because** ....

....

(d) **A** .... **is like a narrow pipe because** ....

....

2 Tamar and Bennie are asked to explain what the battery in the circuit below is doing to make the bulb light.

battery

bulb

Tamar says "The battery supplies charge, and some of it is used in the bulb to make light."
Bennie says "The battery supplies energy and some of it becomes light in the bulb."

(a) Who is right, Tamar or Bennie?

....

(b) Explain your answer to (a).

....

....

Circuit Diagrams

1 Electrical components can be represented by symbols.

(a) Draw the correct circuit symbol for each of the following components.

(i) A cell. (ii) A motor.

(b) Write down the names of the components that have the following symbols.

(i)

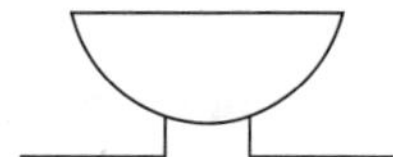

(ii)

....

(c) Explain what the two symbols opposite show.

1 ....

2 ....

2 Electrical circuits can be represented by diagrams.
Draw a circuit diagram for each of the circuits shown below.

(a)

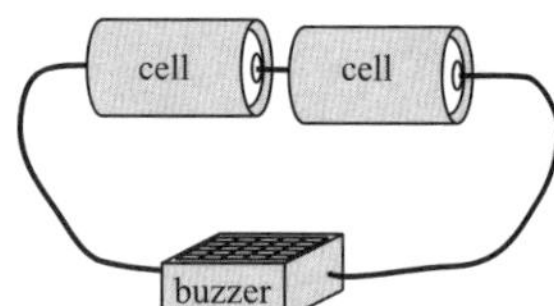

(b)

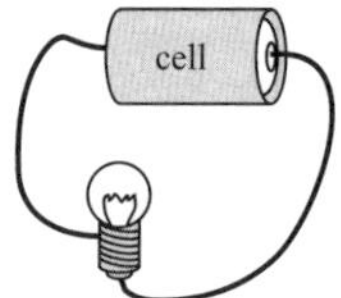

(c)

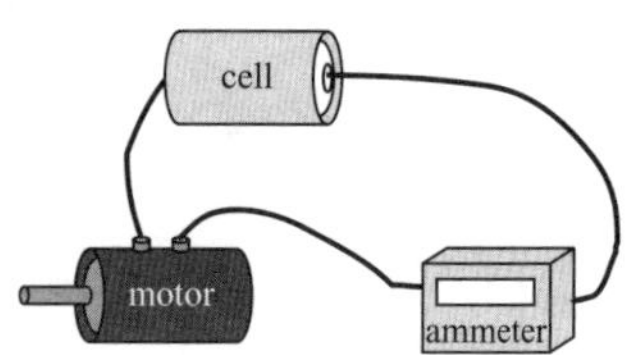

Series Circuits

1 The components in an electrical circuit can be connected in series or in parallel.

(a) Explain what a series circuit is.

....

....

(b) Put a tick below the diagrams that represent series circuits.

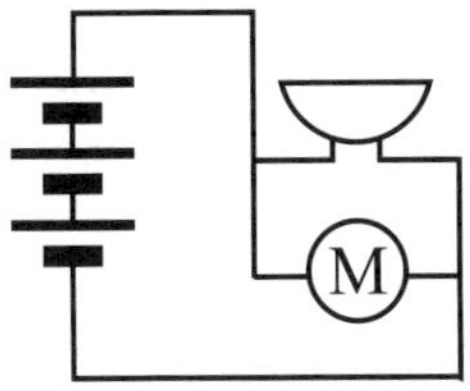

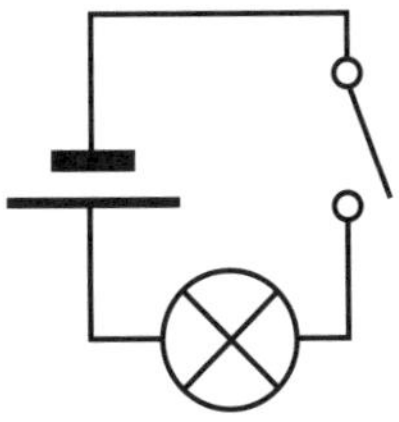

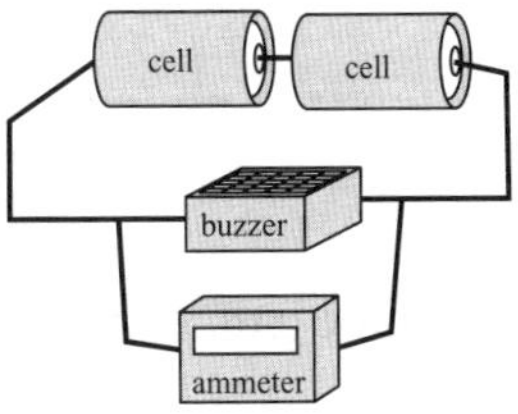

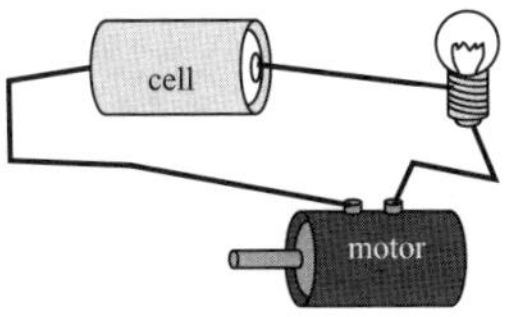

☐ ☐ ☐ ☐

2 An inventor uses a motor and a cell to make a novelty spinning bow tie.

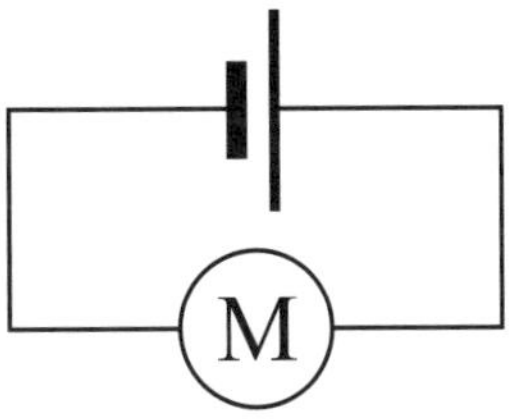

(a) She then adds a buzzer in series with the motor. Will the bow tie spin more quickly, more slowly, or at the same speed? Explain your answer.

....

....

(b) The bow tie suddenly stops spinning, but the buzzer is still working. The inventor decides the motor has been short circuited by another wire round the motor. Explain why a short circuit would stop the motor from working.

....

....

....

Series Circuits

1 Donald has made his own set of battery-powered Christmas tree lights.
A simplified diagram of his circuit is shown below.

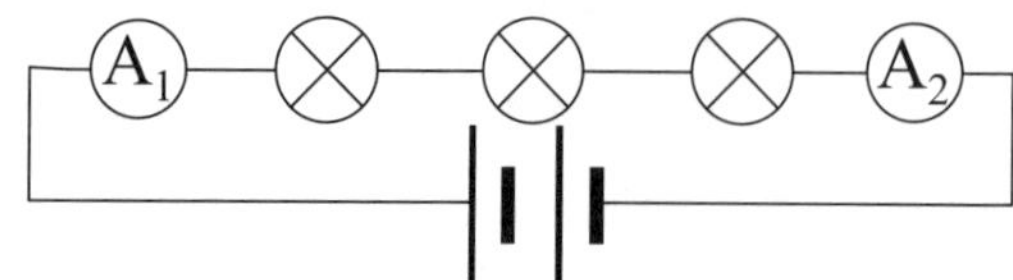

(a) The reading on A_1 is 6.5 A. What will the reading on A_2 be? ....

(b) If one of the bulbs breaks, what effect will this have on the set of lights?

....

2 The current in a series circuit can be measured with a single ammeter.

(a) For each pair of circuits shown below, what will the ammeter read in **circuit 2**?
Explain your answers.

(i)

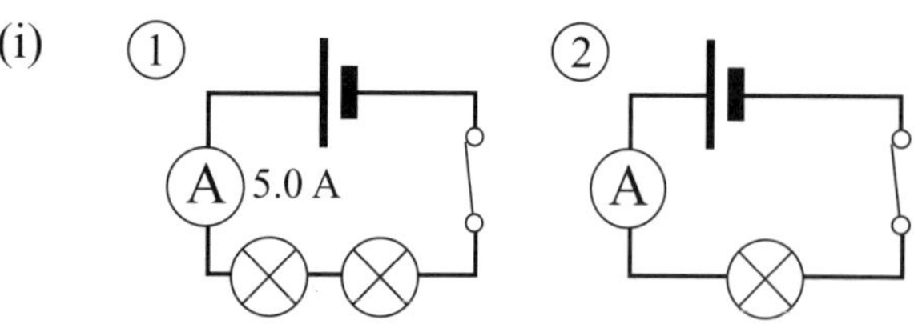

....

....

(ii)

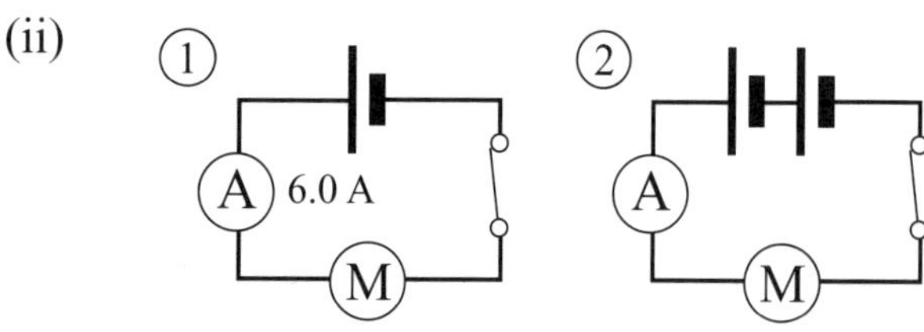

....

....

(b) The ammeter in the circuit below reads 16 A.
Draw **two** different circuits that will have a current of 4 A flowing through them.

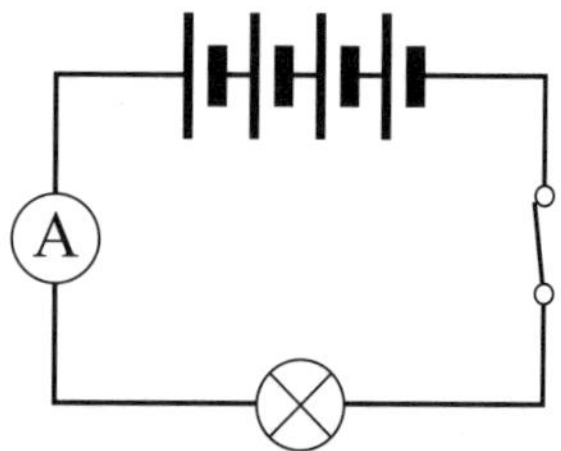

Parallel Circuits

1 The diagram below shows a parallel circuit with a bulb, motor, and four ammeters.

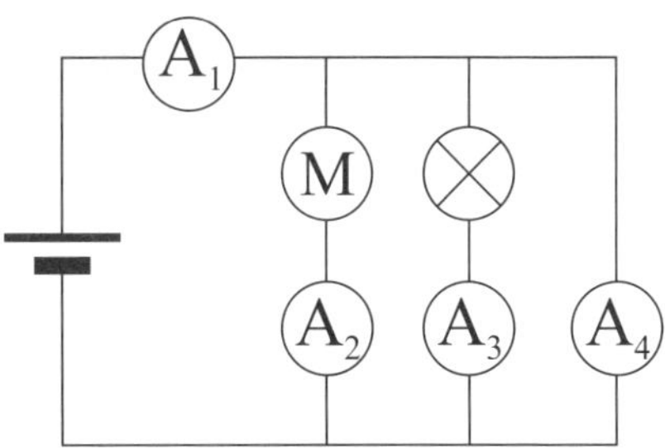

(a) Explain what is meant by a parallel circuit.

....

....

(b) (i) Which ammeter will show how much current is flowing through the **whole circuit** — A_1, A_2, A_3 or A_4? ....

(ii) Which ammeter will show how much current is flowing through the **bulb** — A_1, A_2, A_3 or A_4? ....

(c) (i) Which ammeter would you expect to have the highest reading — A_1, A_2, A_3 or A_4? Explain your answer.

....

....

(ii) Would you expect ammeters A_2, A_3 and A_4 to give the same readings? Explain your answer.

....

....

(iii) Which ammeter would you expect to have the highest reading — A_2, A_3 or A_4? Explain your answer.

....

....

Parallel Circuits

1 The parallel circuit shown on the right contains a motor, a bulb, a buzzer and some ammeters.

(a) Complete the table below to show all the ammeter readings.

Ammeter	1	2	3	4	5
Reading (A)	8	2	5		

(b) The same circuit is set up, but using different components. It is realised that one of the new ammeters is faulty. Use the readings below to work out which one it is.

Ammeter	1	2	3	4	5
Reading (A)	9	3	5	2	10

Ammeter .... is faulty.

2 The circuit below contains three bulbs and four switches. Complete the table to show how the bulbs can be controlled by the switches. The first one has been done for you.

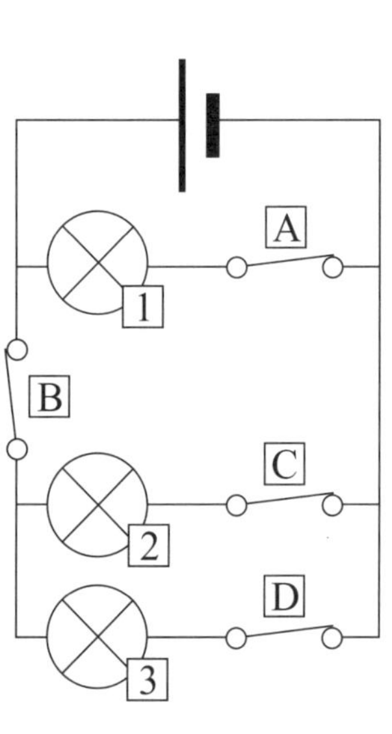

Switches				Bulbs		
A	B	C	D	1	2	3
open	closed	closed	closed	off	on	on
closed	open	closed	closed	on	off	off
closed	closed	open	closed	on	off	on
closed	closed	closed	open	on	on	off
closed	closed	open	open	on	off	off
closed	open	open	closed	on	off	off
closed	closed	closed	closed	on	on	on

Magnets

1 Jordan is using a compass to investigate the magnetic field around a bar magnet.
He places the compass at various positions around the magnet.

(a) Explain what is meant by a **magnetic field**.

....

....

(b) (i) Describe what will happen to the needle of a compass in a magnetic field.

....

....

(ii) Jordan has recorded his first result on the diagram below. Complete it to show what the compass will look like at all the other positions around the magnet.

S N

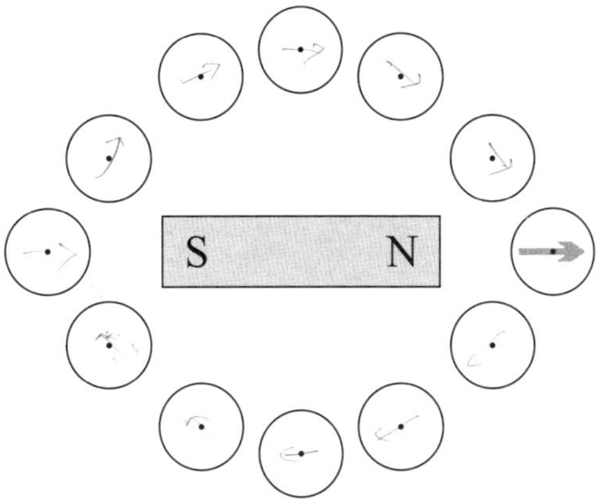

(c) Suggest another way, apart from using a compass, that Jordan can show the magnetic field around a magnet.

....

....

(d) Complete the diagram below to show the field lines around a bar magnet.

S N

Magnets

1 Kirsty knows that a magnet is made by putting a piece of metal in a strong magnetic field. She tries this out with a copper rod, then tests it by holding it near some steel paperclips. The paperclips are not attracted to the copper rod. She tries again using a piece of iron, and this time the paperclips stick to the iron bar.

(a) (i) Why wasn't Kirsty able to make a magnet with a copper rod?

....

(ii) Name **two** other metals, apart from iron, that Kirsty could use to make a magnet.

1 .... 2 ....

(b) Because the paperclips stick to the iron, Kirsty decides she has made a magnet.

(i) Explain why Kirsty may be wrong to decide that the iron has become a magnet.

....

....

(ii) Describe what Kirsty should do to test if the iron has become a magnet.

....

....

2 Peter uses one bar magnet to push another one along the tabletop, then to pull it. Complete the diagrams below to show all the ways the poles could have lined up.

(a) One magnet pushing the other.

S N		or		

(b) One magnet pulling the other.

S N		or		

Electromagnets

1 Rajesh is trying to make an electromagnet.

(a) With the help of a diagram, describe an electromagnet that would be simple for Rajesh to make.

....

....

(b) Give **two** ways Rajesh could increase the strength of this electromagnet.

1 ....

2 ....

(c) Explain why Rajesh should **not** use steel to make the core of the electromagnet.

....

2 The circuit used for an alarm bell is shown below. It contains an electromagnet.

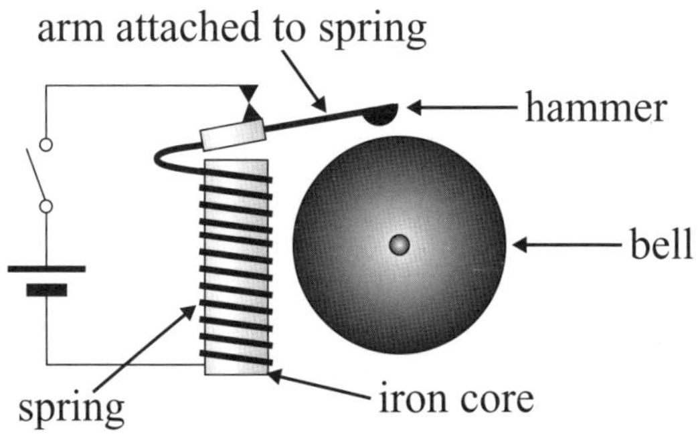

(a) Explain how the circuit makes the bell ring continuously when the switch is closed.

....

....

....

(b) Give **two** reasons why an electromagnet and not a permanent magnet is used in the circuit.

1 ....

2 ....

Electromagnets

1 The design for a switch-operated electric hand drier is shown below.

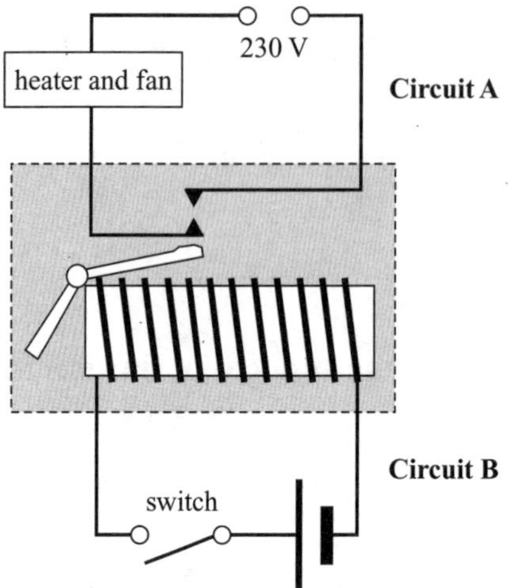

(a) (i) What name is given to the component in the shaded box?

....

(ii) What is this component used for?

....

(b) The design contains two circuits, A and B. One can be described as an input circuit and the other as an output circuit.

(i) Which is which?

Circuit .... is an input circuit. Circuit .... is an output circuit.

(ii) Explain your answer to (i).

....

(c) Describe what will happen when the switch is closed.

....

....

(d) Why is it an advantage to use a design like this one for an electric hand-drier, with two circuits rather than a switch directly connected to the mains?

....

....

Electricity and Magnetism Mini-Exam

1 Rebecca is testing different materials to see whether they will carry an electric current.

(a) (i) What is an electric current?

....

....

(ii) What term is used to describe materials that will carry an electric current?

....

Rebecca uses a cell, a buzzer and some wires to make a circuit to test the materials.

(b) To make sure the buzzer works, she connects it directly to the cell.
Show this circuit in a circuit diagram.

Rebecca then connects various materials into the circuit
and checks whether the buzzer still works.

(c) To find out if the materials will carry an electric current, should she
connect them in series or in parallel? Explain your answer.

....

....

(d) (i) Name **three** substances for which the buzzer will still work.

1 .... 2 ....

3 ....

(ii) Name **three** substances that will **stop** the buzzer from working.

1 .... 2 ....

3 ....

Electricity and Magnetism Mini-Exam

2 Ted puts a copper tube in the middle of a solenoid and connects the solenoid to a battery. The current passing through the solenoid creates a magnetic field.

(a) (i) What is a solenoid?

....

(ii) What has Ted made?

....

(b) (i) Complete the diagram below to show the field lines around the solenoid.

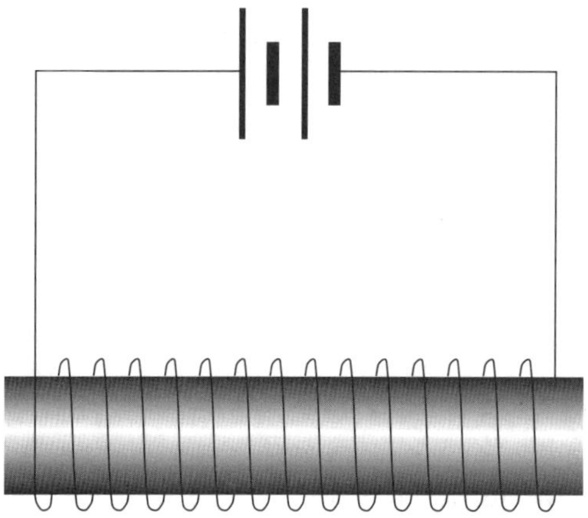

(ii) Ted disconnects the battery from the circuit and reconnects it with its poles the other way round. How will the magnetic field be affected by this?

....

Ted finds that the magnetic field is strong enough to pick up five paperclips.

(c) Suggest **three** things Ted could do to increase the number of paperclips picked up.

1 ....

2 ....

3 ....

Electricity and Magnetism Mini-Exam

(d) (i) Suggest **two** materials that the paperclips might be made of.

1 .... 2 ....

(ii) Explain your answer to (i).

....

....

Ted adds a switch to the circuit in three different places, making three different circuits. These are shown in the diagram below.

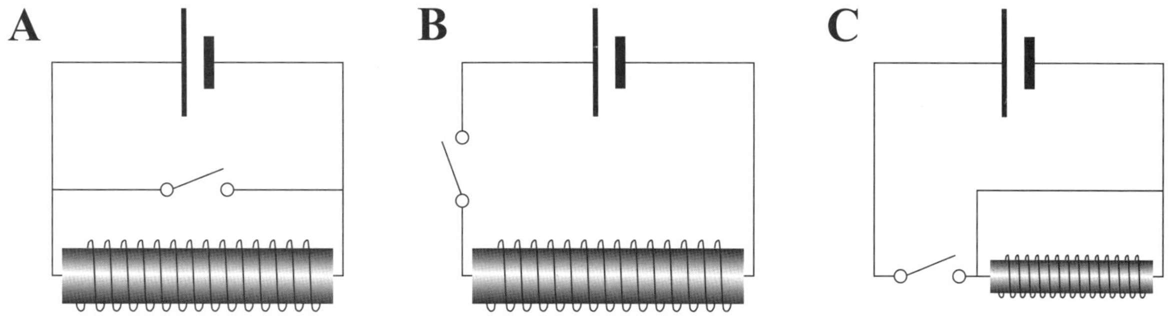

A B C

(e) In which circuits is the switch connected in series? Write their letters below.

....

(f) In which circuit will **closing** the switch reduce the magnetic field?

....

(g) (i) In which circuit will little or no magnetic field be created, whether the switch is open or closed? Explain why.

....

....

....

(ii) What is this effect called?

....

Electricity and Magnetism Mini-Exam

3 Claire has bought three identical decorative lights for her new living room. She wants to connect them so that they work on mains electricity, so that they are on the same switch, and so that if any light fails, the others will carry on working.

(a) Complete the diagram below to show a circuit Claire could use for her new lights.

(b) Claire also needs to add a fuse to her circuit.
This is a safety device included in all circuits connected to mains electricity.
If there is a dangerous increase in the current flowing, it melts and shuts off the current.
Should Claire connect the fuse in series or in parallel? Explain your answer.

....

....

....

4 The circuit below contains four identical bulbs. Ammeter A_1 reads 12 A.

(a) What are the readings on the other ammeters?

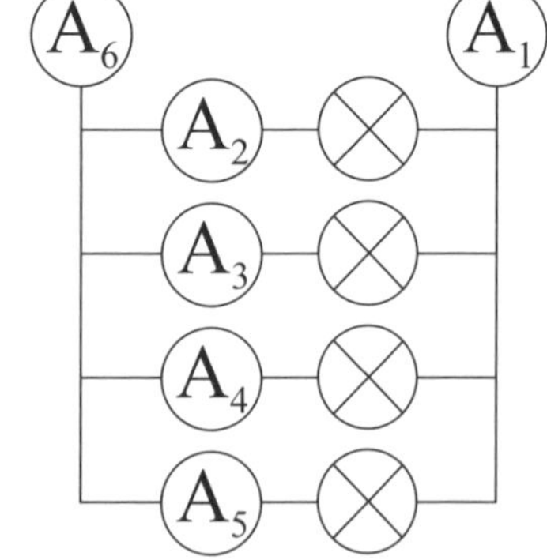

A_2 .... **A_5** ....

A_3 .... **A_6** ....

A_4 ....

(b) Has any current been used up in the circuit?
Explain how you know.

....

(c) Where does the light energy given out by the bulbs come from?

....

Speed

1 A new racing car is being tested to find its top speed by driving it along a straight track. There are two posts on the track, 1 mile apart.

(a) During one test run, the car takes 60 seconds to move between the two posts. What is its speed in miles/hour?

....

(b) The makers of the car have predicted that the car's top speed will be 200 miles/hour.

(i) If the car travels at 200 miles/hour, how long will it take to pass between the posts, in hours?

....

(ii) How long will it take in seconds?

....

(c) At a constant speed of 120 miles/hour, the car travels the whole length of the track in 3 minutes. How long is the track? Include the unit.

....

2 Chris and Jenny both walked to the same beach, but they took different routes.

Beach
500 m
300 m
Chris
400 m
Jenny

(a) Jenny took 10 minutes to reach the beach. What speed was she travelling at, in km/hour? Show your working.

....

....

(b) Chris walked at 4 km/hour. Did he arrive at the beach before or after Jenny? Show your working.

....

....

Speed

1 A research scientist is investigating the properties of various liquids. He drops a metal ball down a tube filled with one of the liquids and measures the time taken for the ball to pass between two marks on the tube. The marks are 50 cm apart. Some of the results are shown in the table below.

Liquid	Time taken to pass between marks	Speed
A	10 seconds	
B	2 seconds	
C	5 seconds	
D		1.0 m/s
E		2.5 m/s
F		0.4 m/s

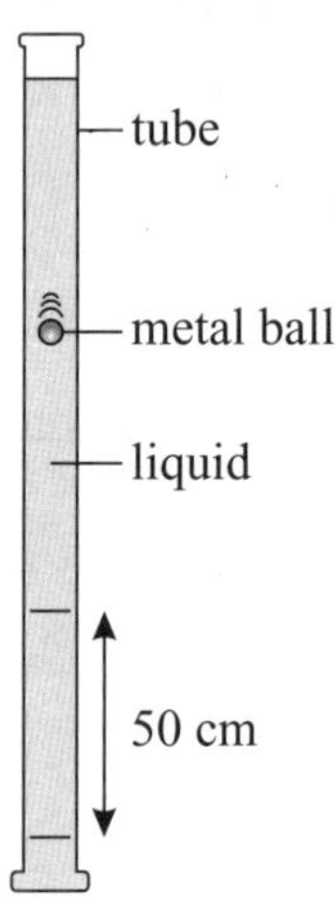

(a) Did the ball drop more quickly through liquid A or through liquid B?

....

(b) What was the speed of the ball when it passed between the marks in liquid C, in metres per second?

....

(c) How long did the ball take to pass between the marks in liquid D?

....

(d) How long would the ball take to pass through 15 m of liquid E?

....

(e) How far through liquid F would the ball travel in 23 seconds?

....

Speed

1 The triathlon is a sport that combines swimming, running and cycling in one race. The graph below shows the speed of one athlete during a triathlon.

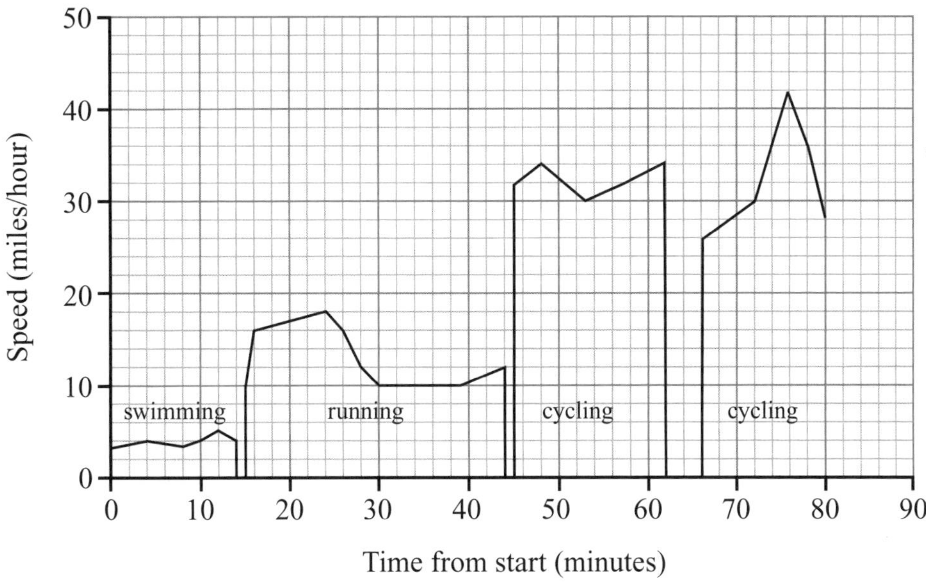

(a) How many minutes after the start of the triathlon was the athlete travelling at her fastest?

....

(b) She had to stop cycling to mend a puncture. For how long did she stop?

....

(c) The athlete ran at a constant speed from 30 minutes to 39 minutes into the race.

(i) How fast was she running during this time?

....

(ii) How far did she run during this time?

....

(d) The athlete's time for the race was 90 minutes. In the last 6 minutes of the race, the athlete travelled 4.4 miles at a constant speed. Complete the **last 6 minutes** on the graph to show this. Use the space below for your working.

....

(e) The athlete cycled for 24 miles in total. What was her **average** cycling speed?

....

Force and Movement

1 The device shown opposite is used to measure forces.
It contains a strong spring and a scale.

(a) (i) What is the name of the device?

....

(ii) What are the units on its scale?

....

The diagram to the right shows a mass hanging from the device.
A pair of forces act on the mass, one upward and one downward.

(b) What is causing

(i) The downward force acting on the mass?

....

(ii) The upward force acting on the mass?

....

(c) The pointer on the scale of the device is not moving.
What can you say about the forces acting on the mass?

....

2 To finish off her cheesecake, Tessa adds a layer of whipped cream and a strawberry on top. There are two forces acting on the strawberry — an upward force from the cream and a downward force of gravity.

What will happen if

(a) The two forces are balanced?

....

(b) The force of gravity is larger than the force from the cream?

....

Force and Movement

1 Each of the pictures below shows a situation where a force is acting on an object. Next to each one, write down the **main** overall effect of the forces on movement. Choose from the following options:

speed up **slow down** **change direction** **turn** **change shape**

(a) A cyclist starts pedalling.

....

(b) The parachute suddenly opens.

....

(c) Cricketer hits a ball.

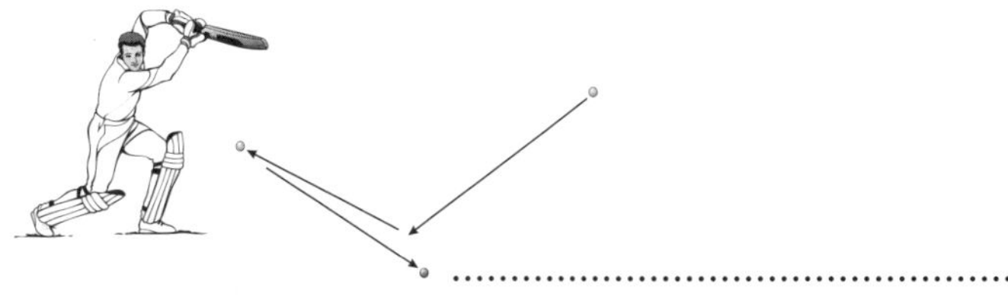

....

2 The diagrams below show a mass hanging from an **elastic** bungee rope after it has been dropped. The force of gravity acts downwards on the mass, and a force from the rope acts upwards. The upward force varies depending on the length of the rope.

A

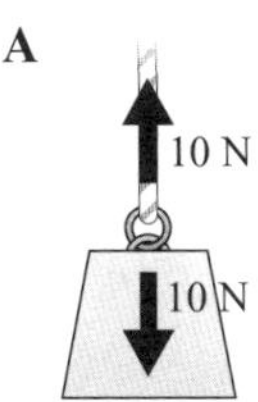

B

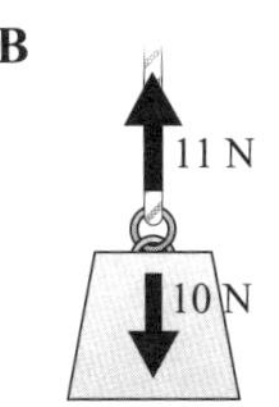

C

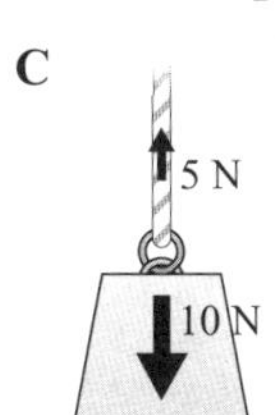

(a) Which diagram — A, B or C — shows the mass when it is

(i) speeding up on the way down? ....

(ii) speeding up on the way up? ....

(iii) not moving? ....

(b) Which diagram shows the mass the longest time after it has been dropped? Explain your answer.

....

....

(c) The weight of the mass is a force that acts on the rope. What effect does this force have on **the rope**?

....

Air Resistance and Friction

1 A skydiver falling through the air has opposing forces acting on him due to gravity and air resistance.

(a) What is air resistance?

....

(b) (i) Describe how the force of air resistance affects the skydiver at the instant he steps out of the plane, before he starts to fall. Explain your answer.

....

....

(ii) The skydiver starts to fall more and more quickly.
What happens to the air resistance acting on him?

....

(c) (i) What happens to air resistance when the skydiver's parachute opens?

....

(ii) Explain why the skydiver falls at a steady speed with the parachute open.

....

....

(d) Write down the letters of the diagrams and labels below in the correct order in the table.

	Diagram	Label
1		
2		
3		
4		
5		

A Steady speed

B Losing speed

C Rapidly gaining speed

D Weight equal to reaction force from ground

E Gradually gaining speed

Air Resistance and Friction

1 Two motorbikes are shown below.

(a) Describe **two** ways in which friction is an **advantage** when riding a motorbike.

1 ....

....

2 ....

....

(b) Describe **two** ways in which friction is a **disadvantage** when riding a motorbike.

1 ....

....

2 ....

....

The motorbikes above have the same mass and the same engine power.

(c) Which do you think will have the higher top speed, A or B? Explain your answer.

....

....

(d) If the motorbikes are travelling at the same speed, suggest which one will use fuel more quickly. Explain your answer.

....

....

Force and Rotation

1 Toby is using a lever to raise a barrel of water.

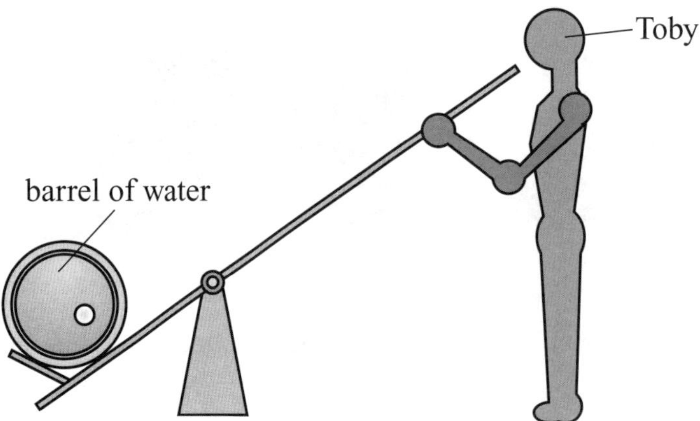

(a) (i) Add **two** arrows to the diagram above to show the **direction** and the **size** (i.e. which force is bigger) of the forces exerted by Toby and by the barrel. Label them **effort force** and **load**.

(ii) Label the diagram to show where the **pivot** is.

(b) What is a pivot?

....

(c) Using the labelled diagram, explain why a lever can be called a machine.

....

....

....

(d) (i) How can Toby reduce the effort he has to put in to lift the barrel, without changing the lever he is using?

....

(ii) Explain your answer to (i).

....

....

Force and Rotation

1 There are many examples of levers in everyday life.

(a) Draw and label arrows to show the direction of the effort force and load, plus the pivot, in each picture below.

(i)

(ii)

nutcracker & walnut

(iii)

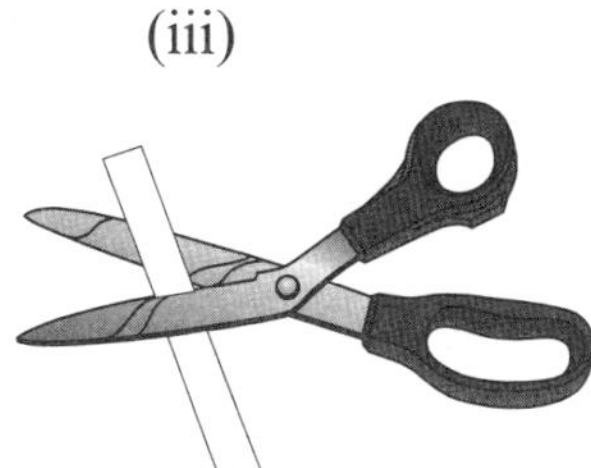

(b) A tool-making company has designed two different wirecutters, shown below.

A

B

(i) Which is the better design, A or B? ....

(ii) Give **two** reasons for your answer to (i).

1 ....

2 ....

2 Gordon and Barry are equally matched at arm wrestling — their hands are not moving.

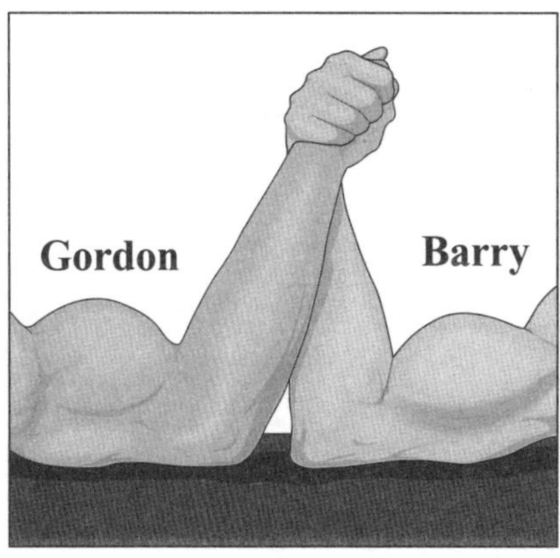

(a) Draw and label two arrows on the picture opposite to show the effort force and load for **Barry**. Both the size and the direction of the forces should be shown.

(b) Compared to the other levers on this page, what is different about the arm as a lever?

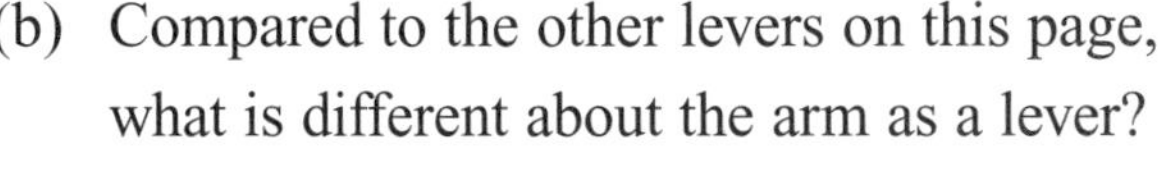

....

....

Moments

1 The diagram below shows a set of scales used to measure rice.
Rice is placed in the dish, and the mass is moved along the arm until the scales balance.

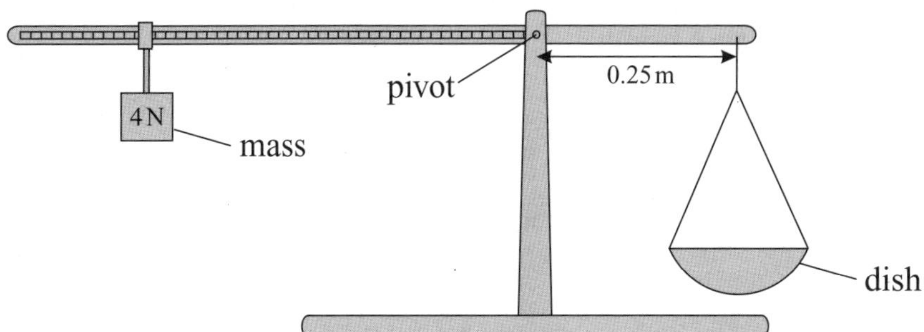

(a) The weight of the rice and of the mass create turning forces about the pivot.

(i) What name is given to a turning force about a pivot?

....

(ii) What are the units used to measure such a turning force?

....

A bag of rice with weight 10 N is placed in the dish.

(b) What turning force will act about the pivot? Show your working and give the units.

....

(c) What distance from the pivot must the mass be placed to balance the scales?
Show your working and give the units.

....

....

(d) What weight of rice will balance the scales if the mass is 10 cm from the pivot?
Show your working and give the units.

....

....

....

Moments

1 Diagram A below shows the structure of Jason's arm. The arm muscles attached to the forearm exert a force that can make the forearm pivot around the elbow. Diagram B is a simplified diagram showing the moments that act about Jason's elbow when he holds an object in his hand.

A

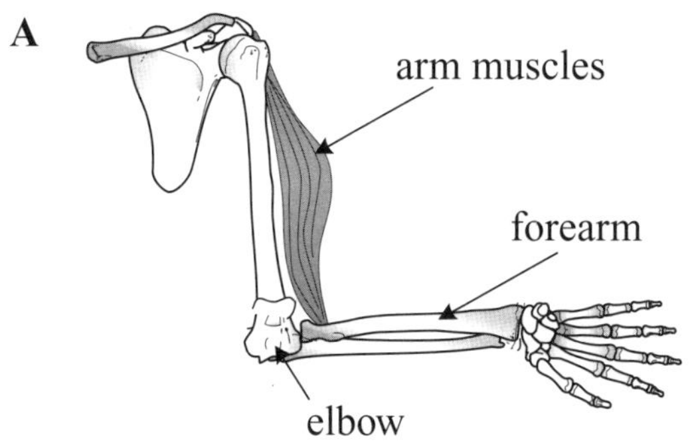

B

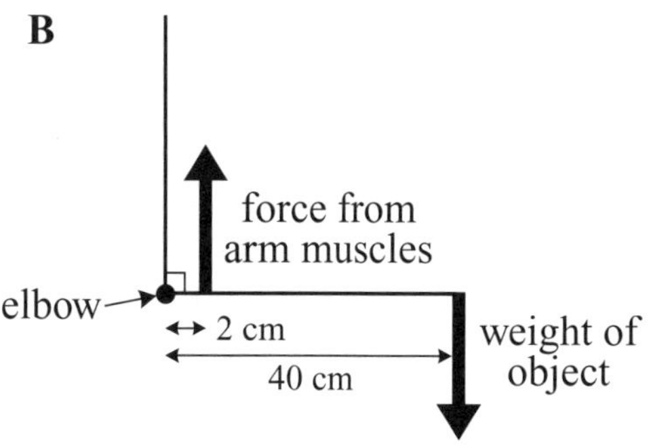

(a) Jason's arm muscles exert a force at 2 cm from the elbow. The largest force that they can exert is 4000 N. What moment will this give about the elbow, in Newton metres?

....

....

(b) (i) Will the maximum weight that Jason can hold steady in his hand be smaller or larger than 4000 N? Explain your answer.

....

....

....

(ii) Calculate the maximum weight that Jason will be able to support in his hand.

....

....

(iii) Jason tries to hold a 220 N weight in his hand. Suggest what will happen.

....

....

Moments

1 Bomb-disposal experts often need to open up a bomb to defuse it.
A remote-controlled 'spanner' can be used to unscrew parts of the bomb at a safe distance.
This uses rockets to supply the turning force.

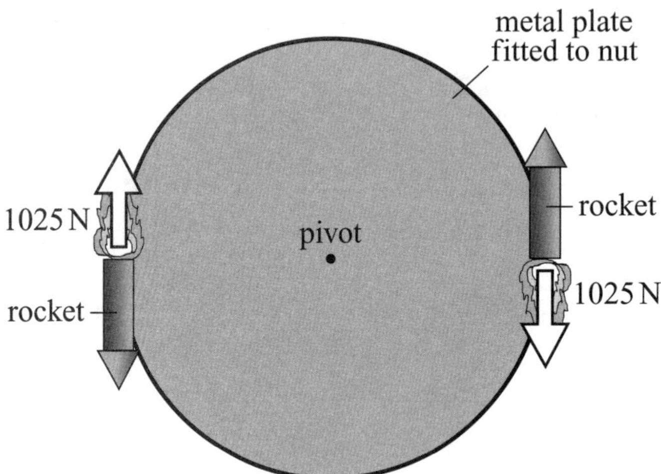

The 'spanner' in the diagram above is set up so that each rocket is 0.1 m from the pivot.
It is being used to unscrew a nut on a Second World War bomb.

(a) (i) At the first attempt to unscrew the nut, one of the rockets fails to fire.
What is the moment created by the other rocket?
Show your working and give the units.

....

(ii) At the second attempt, both rockets fire. What is the moment created?
Show your working and give the units.

....

(b) The nut is not loosened even when both rockets fire. The experts decide to increase the moment to 820 Nm by fixing more rockets to the spanner.

(i) How many rockets are needed to produce this moment?
(Each rocket exerts a force of 1025 Nm at a distance of 0.1 m from the pivot.)

....

....

(ii) How could the bomb-disposal experts increase the moment without using more rockets?

....

Pressure

1 Mairi hammers a nail into a wall with a force of 12 N.

(a) The point of the nail has an area of 0.1 cm^2.
What pressure is exerted by the hammer on the point of the nail

(i) in N/cm^2? Show your working.

....

(ii) in N/m^2? Show your working.

....

(iii) in Pascals?

....

(b) Mairi misses the nail and hits the wall with the hammer.
Explain why the hammer doesn't penetrate the wall, even though the nail does.

....

....

....

2 Max stands with both feet on the floor.
Each foot exerts a pressure of 12 000 Pa on the floor.

(a) What will the pressure on the floor be if Max lifts one foot off the floor?
Explain your answer.

....

....

(b) The area of contact between the soles of Max's feet (with both feet on the floor) and the floor is 0.06 m^2. What does Max weigh? Show your working and give the units.

....

....

Pressure

1 Isobel is arranging a set of four books on her new bookshelves. Each book has the dimensions shown opposite and weighs 27 N.

20 cm
3 cm
27 cm

(a) Which of the two ways of arranging the books shown below will put least pressure on the bookshelf? Show your working.

A

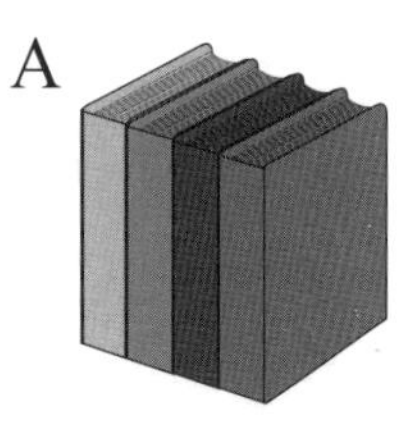

B

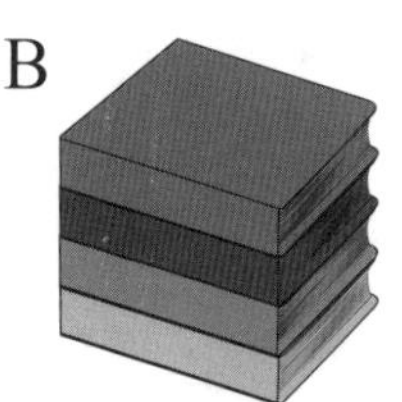

(b) How will arranging the books differently affect the weight the shelf must bear?

2 A company is designing an alarm button that an elderly person can carry with them and use if they need to call for help. The alarm is set off when the plate is pressed hard enough to create a pressure of 4 N/cm^2.

(a) In the first design of the button, the plate has an area of 9 cm^2. What force is needed to set off the alarm?

(b) The designers want to reduce the force needed to set off the alarm to 28 N. What area should they make the plate?

Pressure

1 Anne has bought a statue for her garden, but the ground where she wants to put it is soft. She estimates that if the pressure of the statue on the ground goes over 4000 Pa it will sink.

(a) The statue weighs 450 N and has an area of contact with the ground of 0.06 m^2. Anne thinks it will sink. Is she correct? Show your working.

....

....

(b) She decides to make a base for the statue out of concrete. Explain how adding a base can reduce the pressure of the statue on the ground.

....

....

(c) The base has an area of 0.16 m^2. What is the maximum weight Anne can make the base?

....

....

2 Alan is building a house. The house exerts a force of 240 000 N on the foundations. The foundations spread this load over an area of 8 m^2.

(a) What is the pressure on the foundations?

....

(b) Building laws say that the pressure on the foundations should be not more than 32 000 Pa. How much smaller could Alan have made the area of the foundations without breaking the building laws?

....

....

Forces and Motion Mini-Exam

1 The picture opposite shows a reclining bicycle.
Unlike a standard bicycle, the pedals are in front of the rider, who has to lie back in the seat to reach them.

Various forces act against the bicycle when it moves along, such as air resistance and the resistance of the bicycle's parts to movement.

(a) (i) What type of force are all the forces acting against the movement of the bicycle examples of?

....

(ii) Give **one** way that this type of force is useful to the bicycle's rider.

....

(b) Suggest why the reclining bicycle has a higher top speed than most standard bicycles.

....

At a constant speed, the bicycle takes 12.5 s to travel between two poles 0.15 km apart.
During this time, the force acting against the movement of the bicycle is 120 N.

(c) What is the speed of the bicycle? Show your working and give the units.

....

(d) (i) What is the forward force produced by the rider? Explain how you know.

....

....

(ii) Explain in terms of forces what happens to the movement of the bicycle if the rider reduces the forward force.

....

....

....

Forces and Motion Mini-Exam

2 A simplified diagram of a car's braking system is shown below. The force of the driver's foot on the brake pedal is transferred to the brake pad by a liquid called brake fluid. Force Y is the force of the brake pad on the wheel.

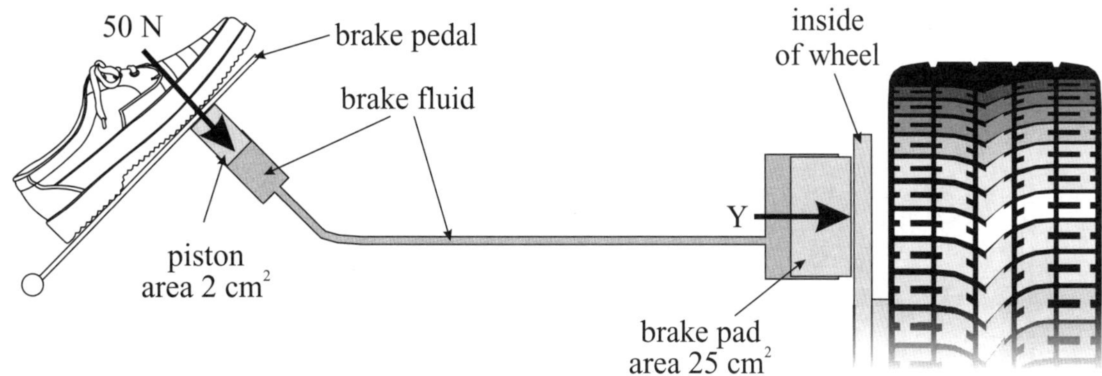

(a) In the diagram above, the driver applies a force of 50 N to the brake pedal.

(i) What is the pressure of the piston on the brake fluid, in N/cm^2?
Show your working.

....

....

(ii) The pressure of the piston on the brake fluid is the same as the pressure of the brake fluid on the brake pad. Calculate force Y, giving the correct units.

....

....

(b) (i) On a hill, the brake pad must produce a braking force of at least 450 N to stop the car from rolling backwards. The perpendicular distance from the brake pad to the centre of the wheel is 0.14 m. What is the smallest moment that will hold the car still? Show your working and give the units.

....

(ii) On another hill, a moment of at least 35 Nm is needed to keep the car still.
What is the minimum braking force that the brake pad must produce?
Show your working and give the units.

....

Forces and Motion Mini-Exam

3 A door is fitted with a closing device to stop the wind blowing it open.
In the diagram below, force W is the force of the wind against the door,
and force C is the force exerted by the closing device. The area of the door is 1.6 m^2.

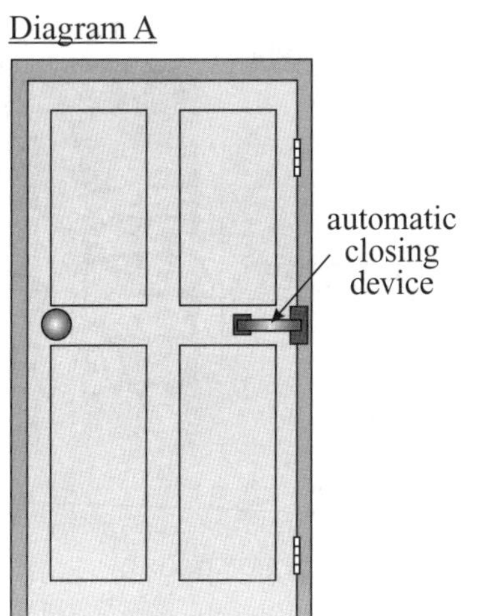

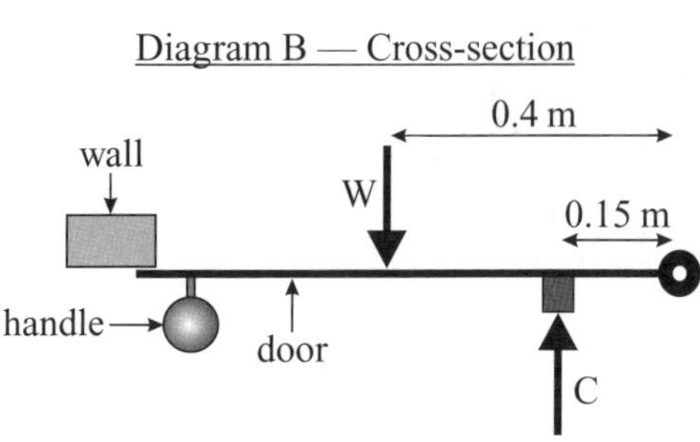

(a) The door acts as a lever.

(i) Label the **pivot** on diagram B.

(ii) Which of the two forces is the **effort force** and which is the **load**?

Force W is the ....

Force C is the ....

(b) A wind blowing at 5 m/s exerts a pressure of 20 Pa on the door.

(i) What is the force of the wind against the door? Show your working.

....

(ii) The force of the wind acts at a perpendicular distance of 0.4 m from the pivot.
Calculate the moment of the force about the pivot.

....

(iii) The moment produced by the closing device about the pivot is 10 Nm.
Will the door be blown open by the wind? Explain your answer.

....

....

....

Forces and Motion Mini-Exam

Jessica is pulling on the door so that it stays partly open.
In the diagram below, force C is the force exerted by the closing device and force J is the force exerted by Jessica pulling on the door handle.

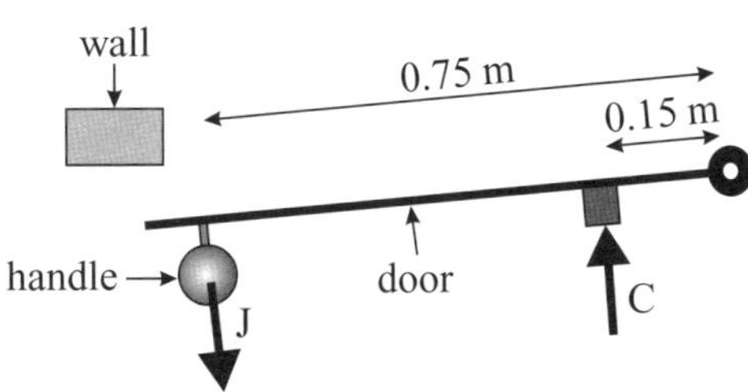

(c) Force C is 10 N. What is the moment of force C about the pivot?
Show your working.

....

(d) (i) What is the moment of force J about the pivot? Explain how you know.

....

(ii) Calculate the value of force J, in newtons.

....

(e) Explain the relationship between force J and force C.

....

....

(f) What will happen to the movement of the door if force J

(i) **increases?** ....

(ii) **decreases?** ....

(g) The makers of the closing device decide to change the design to produce a larger moment about the pivot. Describe **two** ways they could do this.

1 ....

2 ....

Properties of Light

1 Charmaine enters a darkened room, and switches on a table lamp.
There is a mug on the table in front of her.

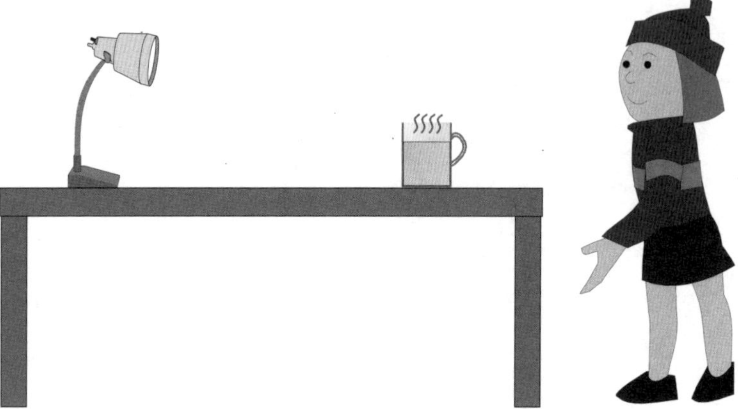

(a) (i) Draw a ray of light on the diagram above to show how Charmaine is able to see the light bulb in the table lamp.

(ii) Using the diagram you completed in (i), explain how Charmaine is able to see the light bulb.

....

....

(iii) Name **two** other objects (not visible in the diagram) that Charmaine would be able to see in the same way.

1 .... 2 ....

(b) (i) Draw a ray of light on the diagram above to show how Charmaine is able to see the mug on the table.

(ii) Name **two** other objects (not visible in the diagram) that Charmaine would be able to see in the same way.

1 .... 2 ....

(iii) Why wouldn't Charmaine be able to see the mug without switching on the lamp?

....

....

Properties of Light

1 The pinhole camera in the diagram below is used to trace an image of a tree.

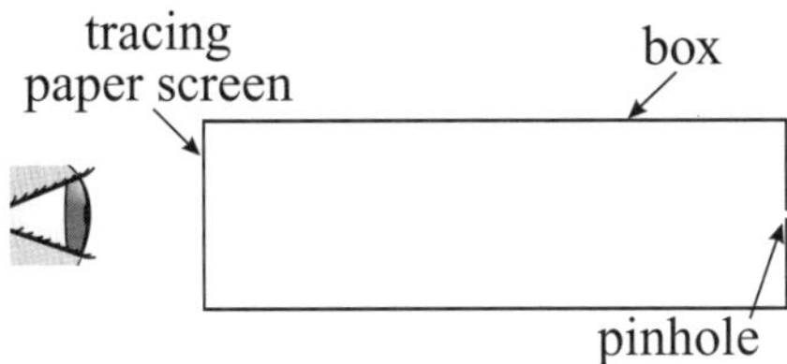

(a) Draw lines to show how the image of the tree is formed on the tracing paper screen.

(b) Explain why the image of the tree appears upside down.

....

....

2 Arif and Pritti are watching a firework display at their local park.

(a) The display takes place at night, and there are very few lights in the park.

(i) Explain why Arif and Pritti can see the fireworks explode even though it is dark.

....

(ii) Suggest how their view of the fireworks would be affected if there were more lights in the park. Explain your answer.

....

....

(b) They hear the explosions of the fireworks a short time after they see them, and Arif hears the explosions about a second after Pritti does.

(i) Who is watching the display from further away, Arif or Pritti? Explain how you know.

....

(ii) Arif and Pritti see the fireworks explode at the same time. Using your answer to (i), suggest how the speed of light compares to the speed of sound.

....

....

Reflection

1 The diagram below shows a ray of light hitting a mirror.

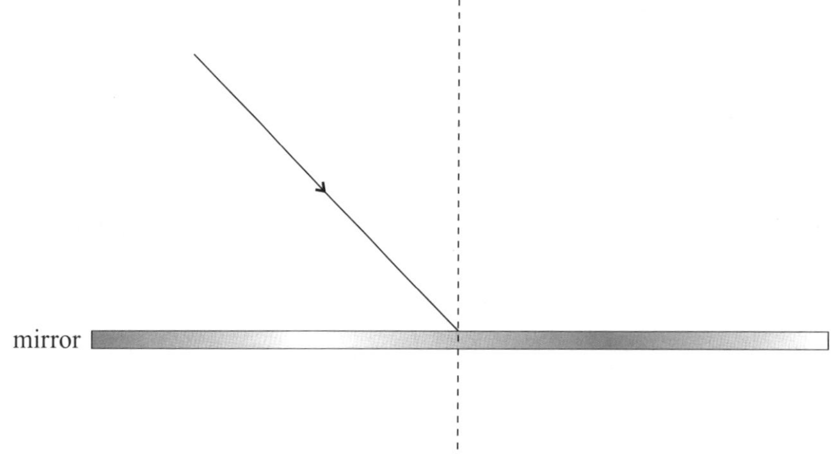

(a) Label the diagram with the correct **names** for the following.

(i) The ray of light travelling to the mirror. (ii) The dotted line.

(b) On the diagram, draw

(i) The angle of incidence, **i**.

(ii) The reflected light ray.

(iii) The angle of reflection, **r**.

(c) The diagram above is an example of the law of reflection.

(i) What is the law of reflection?

....

....

(ii) Explain why the light falling on a mirror obeys the law of reflection.

....

....

(iii) Describe a situation where the light falling on an object does not obey the law of reflection.

....

....

Reflection

1 Claire is using a periscope to see Johan, who is standing on the other side of the wall.

(a) What property of light means that Claire is not able to see Johan without the periscope?

....

(b) Complete the diagram above, by

(i) drawing the two mirrors in Claire's periscope.

(ii) drawing a ray of light to show how the periscope allows Claire to see Johan.

2 A sheet of paper will reflect much more light than a sheet of glass.

(a) (i) Suggest what will happen to the light falling on a sheet of glass that is not reflected.

....

(ii) Explain why a sheet of glass gives a clear reflection.

....

....

(b) (i) What term is used to describe the type of reflection that happens when light hits a sheet of paper?

....

(ii) Explain why a sheet of paper does not give a clear reflection.

....

....

Reflection

1 Mirrors have been used in theatres to make 'ghosts' appear on stage. The diagram below shows how this can be done.

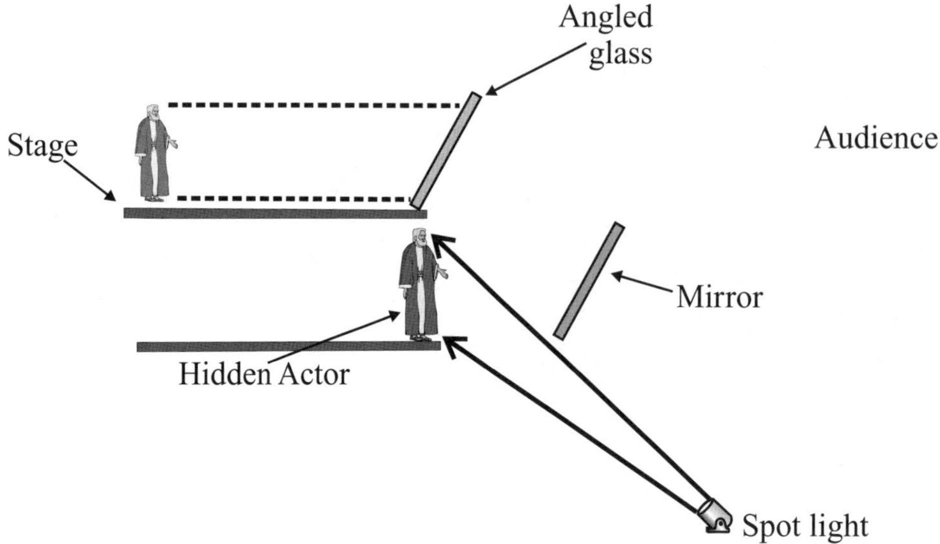

(a) Complete the two rays of light in the diagram to show how the image of the ghost reaches the audience.

(b) The ghost can be made to disappear. Suggest how this is done.

....

(c) Explain why the sheet of angled glass on the stage can be described as a **two-way mirror**.

....

....

....

(d) Describe **three** other uses for mirrors.

1 ....

2 ....

3 ....

Refraction

1 Light rays can be bent when they pass from one medium to another.

(a) (i) All the media (substances) that light can pass between have one property in common. What is it?

....

(ii) What name is given to the bending of light when it passes between media?

....

(b) Explain why light is bent when it passes from one medium to another.

....

....

....

(c) Complete the diagrams below to show the path taken by a ray of light as it passes from air into the glass blocks and back into air.

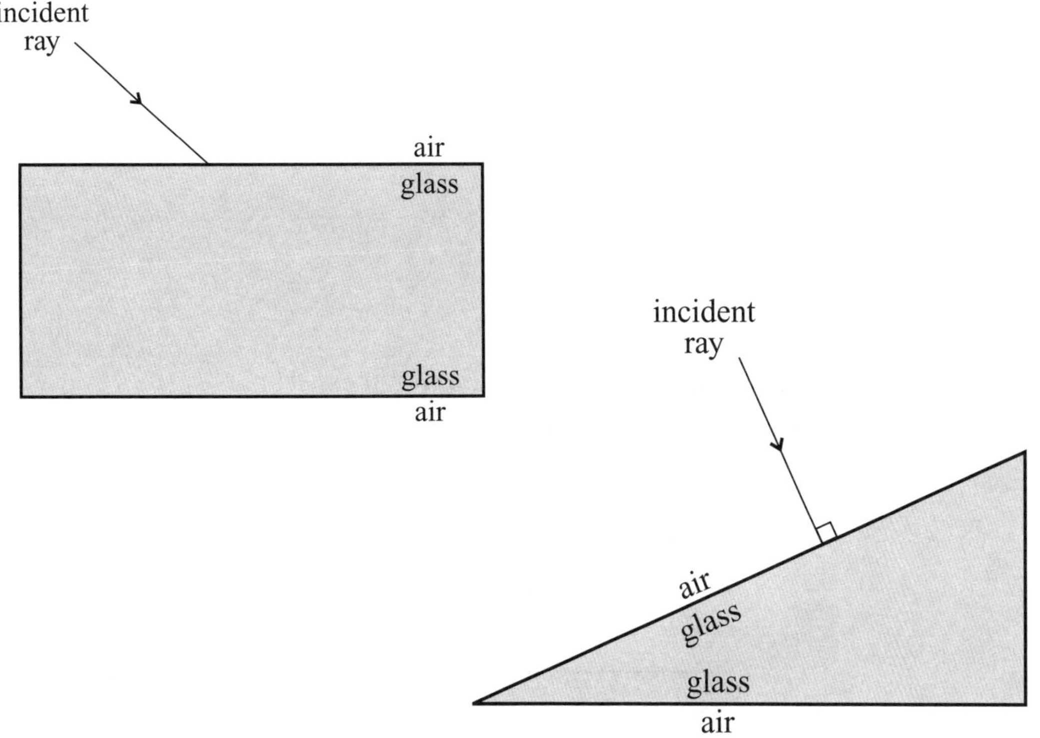

Refraction

1 Lesley is investigating how much light bends when it passes between different media. She sets up two experiments. In the first one, she shines a ray of light so that it travels from air into water. In the second one, the ray travels from air into glass.

(a) Name **one** thing that Lesley should keep the same in both experiments so that she can compare the results.

....

The diagram below shows Lesley's results.

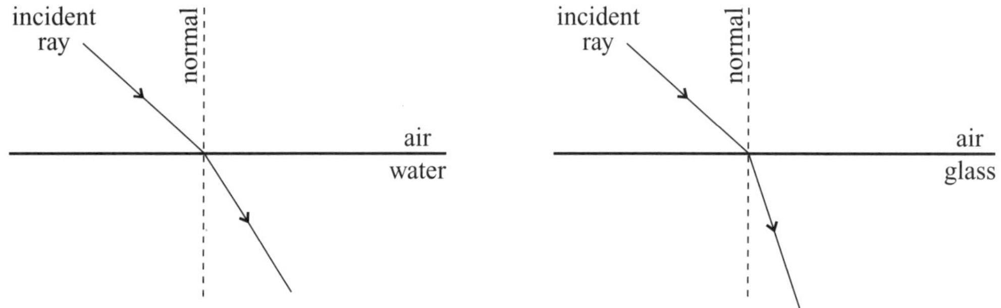

(b) Does light travel more quickly through **water** or **glass**? Explain your answer.

....

....

....

(c) Complete the diagram below to show how you would expect light to bend as it travels from **water** to **glass**.

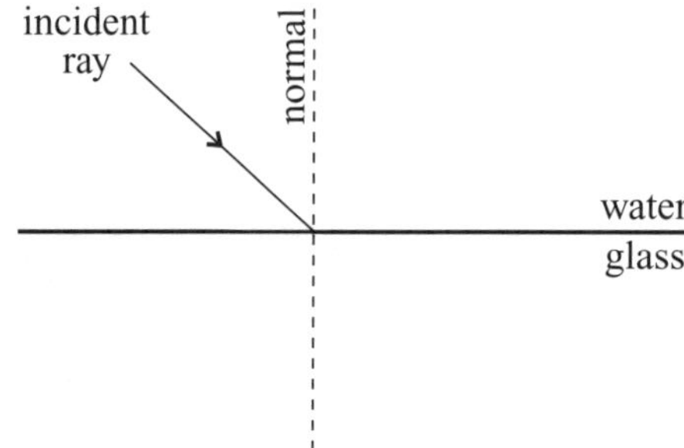

Refraction

1 Tariq asks Drew to stand at a particular spot in the room, and look at a bowl on the table in front of him. There is a coin in the bowl, but Drew can't see it from where he's standing. Tariq then carefully pours some water into the bowl, and the coin 'appears'.

(a) What property of the material the bowl is made out of means that Drew can't see the coin until Tariq pours the water in?

....

In the diagram below, the dotted lines show how Drew sees the coin as if the light rays were travelling in a straight line.

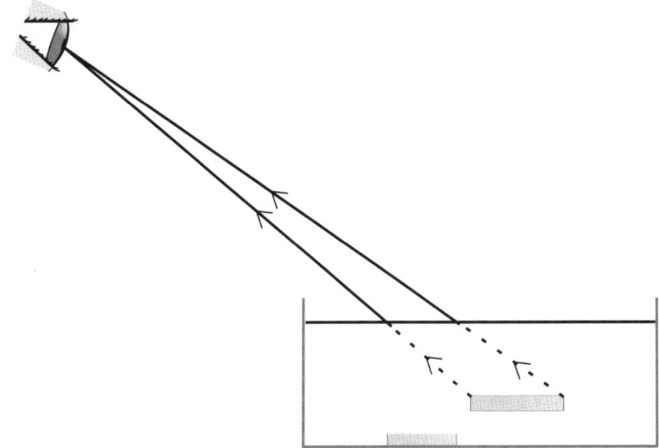

(b) Complete the diagram to show the path the light rays actually take.

(c) Use the completed diagram to answer the following questions.

(i) Should a fisherman on a riverbank aim to cast his bait beyond, before or straight at the place he sees a fish?

....

(ii) Explain why, when you are standing on the side of a swimming pool, it is always deeper than it looks.

....

....

....

....

Colour

1 When white light shines on a glass prism it bends and is split up into different colours. In the diagram below, a rainbow pattern appears on the screen.

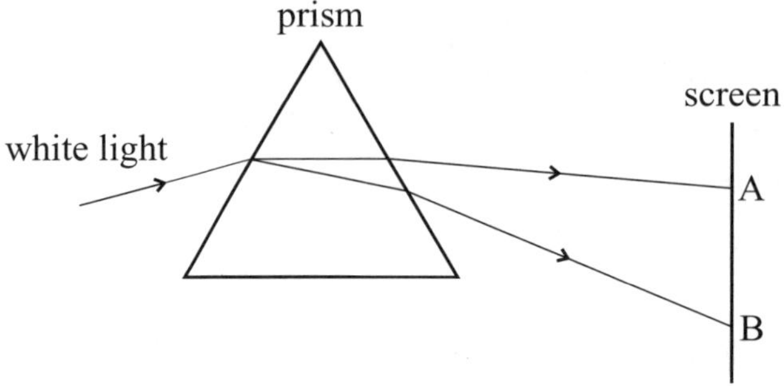

(a) What term is used to describe

(i) The rainbow pattern on the screen?

....

(ii) The splitting of light into different colours?

....

(b) (i) Name the colour that appears at A on the screen.

....

(ii) Name the colour that appears at B on the screen.

....

(iii) Explain why the different colours split up when white light is shone on a prism.

....

....

....

(c) A rainbow sometimes forms when it rains. Explain how this happens.

....

....

....

Colour

1 Eric sets up the four experiments shown below to investigate how different colours of filters and light can change the way objects look. He uses a poppy from his garden. In daylight it has a red flower and green leaves. He also uses a magenta filter, which absorbs all colours of light except red and blue and a blue filter, which absorbs all colours of light except blue.

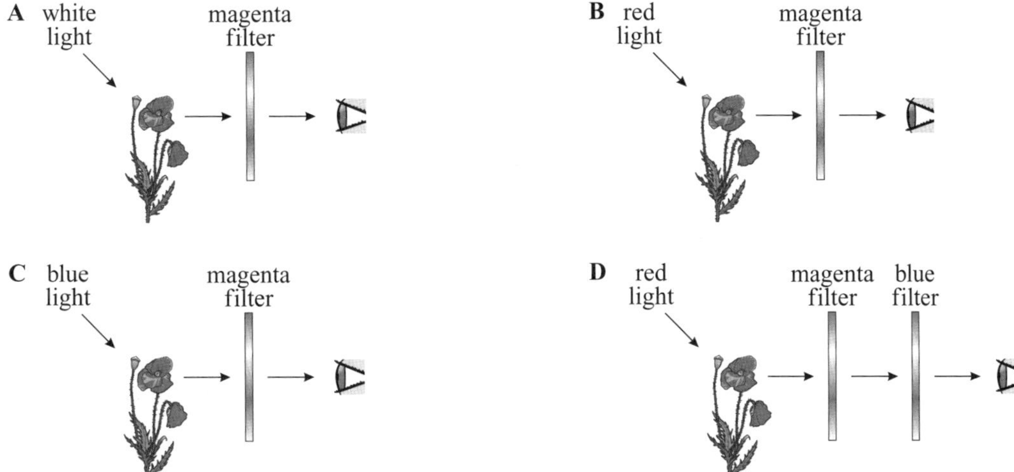

(a) For each experiment, say what colour the poppy **flower** will appear to be when Eric looks at it through the filter, and explain your answer.

A Colour .... **Explanation** ....

....

B Colour .... **Explanation** ....

....

C Colour .... **Explanation** ....

....

D Colour .... **Explanation** ....

....

(b) What colour will the poppy's **leaves** appear in all the experiments? Explain your answer.

....

....

Sound

1 Joel and Zach are astronauts. They are working on the outside of a new space station, which means they have to work in the vacuum of space.

(a) Explain why Joel and Zach can see each other but must use radios to hear each other.

....

....

(b) Joel's radio fails. Describe how the sound of Zak's voice is able to reach Joel if they put their helmets together so that they touch.

....

....

2 Yasmin stands at the mouth of a cave and claps her hands. She hears the sound twice, first at the time she claps her hands and then again a few moments later.

(a) (i) What term is used to describe the sound when Yasmin hears it the second time?

....

(ii) What happened to the sound that means she hears it a second time?

....

(b) Explain why there is a delay before Yasmin hears the sound for the second time.

....

(c) The second time Yasmin hears the sound it is fainter. Suggest why.

....

(d) Yasmin knows that sound travels at about 300 m/s.
Suggest how she could use this information to estimate the size of the cave.

....

....

Sound

1 Ivan is using an oscilloscope connected to a microphone to investigate sounds. He plays three notes on his violin, and obtains traces of the sound waves he makes. The traces are shown below. They all have the same amplitude.

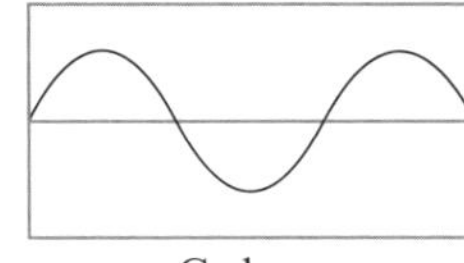
G sharp

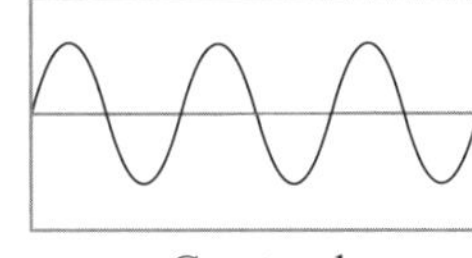
C natural

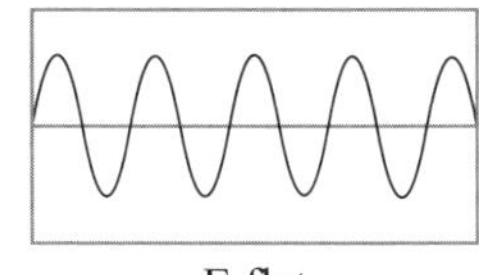
E flat

(a) Explain what is meant by the amplitude of a wave.

....

(b) All the notes Ivan plays have a different pitch. In what way do they sound similar?

....

(c) Ivan plays another note, and this time the trace has a smaller amplitude.
Describe **two** changes in the experiment that could have made the amplitude smaller.

1 ....

2 ....

2 Oscilloscope traces were obtained for the following sounds using the same oscilloscope settings.

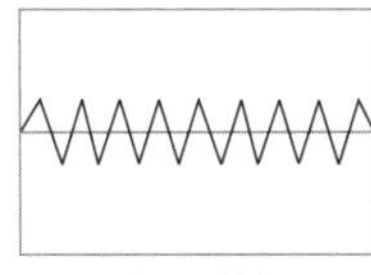
quiet talking

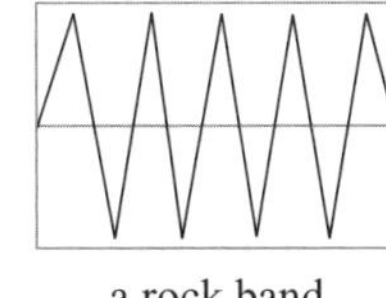
a rock band

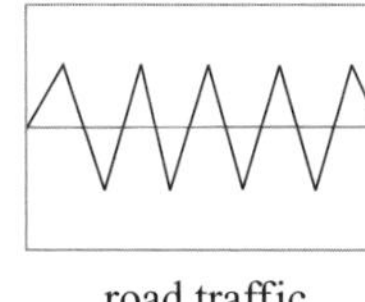
road traffic

(a) (i) Which of the sounds was loudest? Explain how you know.

....

....

(ii) Explain why this sound was loudest.

....

(b) On the oscilloscope screen on the right, draw how you would expect the trace for the sound of a whisper to look.

Sound

1 The oscilloscope traces for sound waves with different frequencies are shown below.

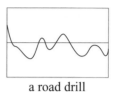

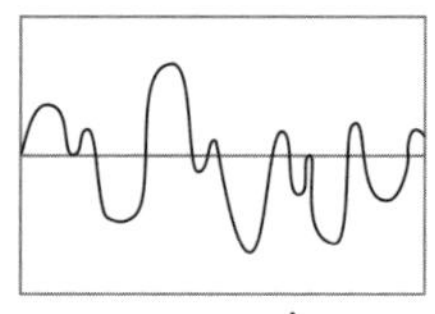
a car engine

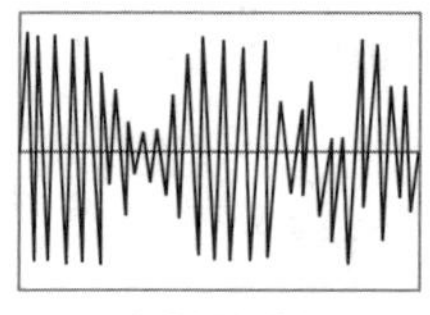
a scream

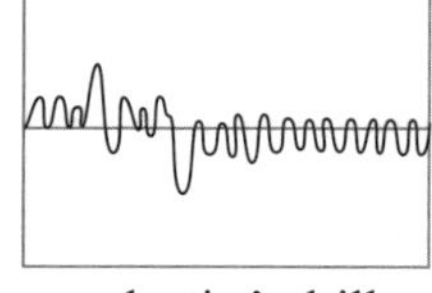
a dentist's drill

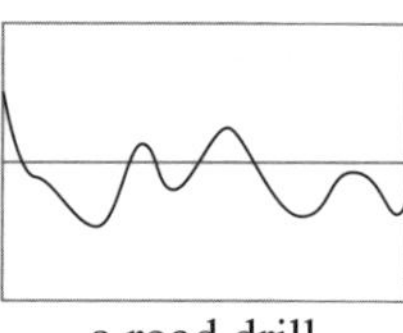
a road drill

(a) (i) What is meant by the frequency of a wave?

....

(ii) Describe the relationship between frequency and the way a noise sounds.

....

(b) Write the noises shown in the diagram above in order of frequency, lowest first.

1 .... 2 ....

3 .... 4 ....

2 Abdul has a new mobile phone, with four different ring tones to choose from.
The oscilloscope traces for the ring tones are shown below.

A
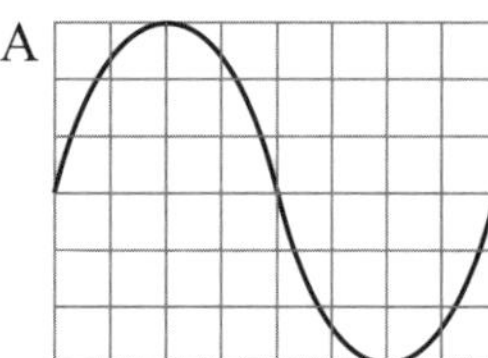

B
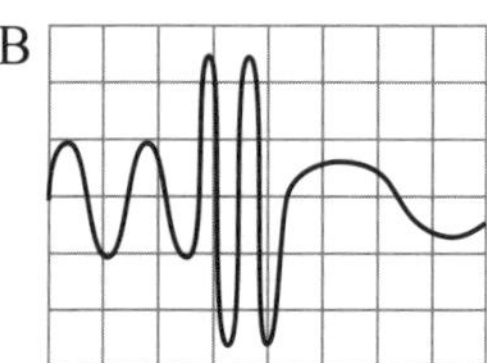

C
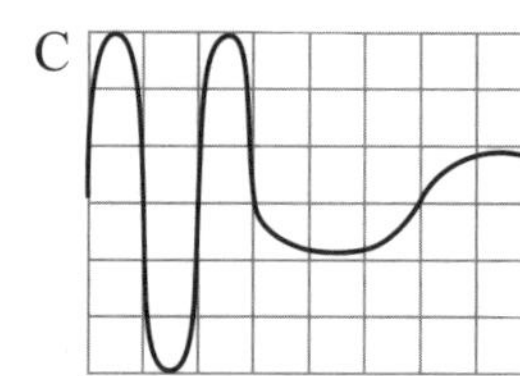

D
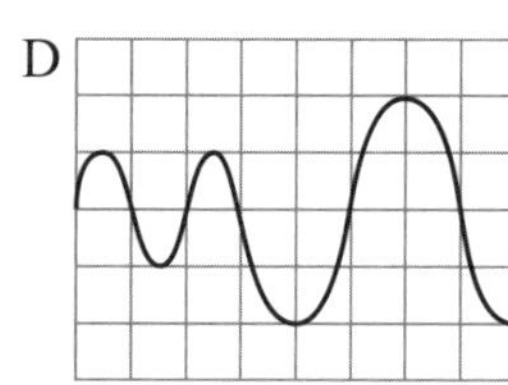

(a) Which ring tone has three notes in it? Explain how you know.

....

(b) Which ring tone contains the lowest note? ....

(c) Abdul decides to program the phone with his own ring tone.
It has two notes. The first note is the same as in A above.
The second note is twice the frequency of the first.
On the oscilloscope screen opposite, draw what the trace
for Abdul's ring tone might look like.

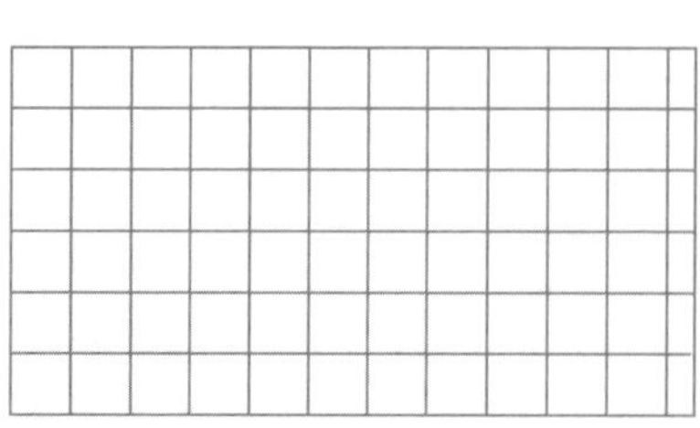

Hearing

1 Julie whispers to Heather during a lesson.

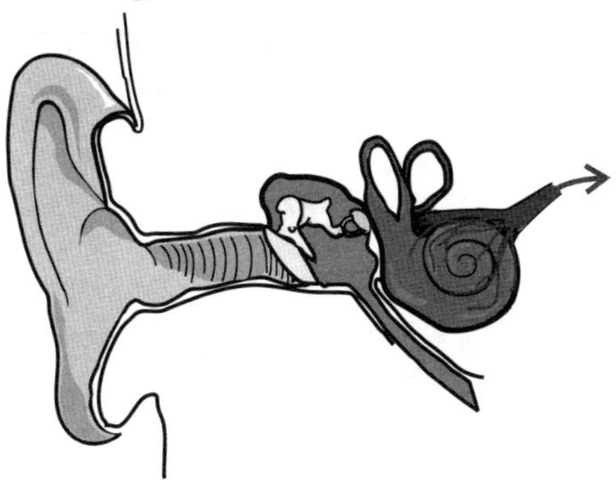

(a) Label the following parts of Heather's ear on the diagram above.

semi-circular canals **ear drum** **cochlea**
ear bones **Eustachian tube** **auditory nerve**

(b) When Julie whispers, the vocal cords in her throat vibrate.
Use the diagram to help you describe what happens to these vibrations so that Heather hears them as the sound of Julie's whisper.

....

....

....

....

(c) The table opposite shows the loudness of some sounds.

Sound	Loudness (dB)
Quietest sound it is possible to hear	1
Quiet talking	40
A busy classroom	70

(i) What does dB stand for?

....

(ii) Use the table to estimate the loudness of Julie's whisper.

....

(iii) The teacher is standing next to Julie.
Suggest why Heather hears Julie's whisper but the teacher does not.

....

....

Hearing

1 Matthew is carrying out an experiment to find the audible range of pitch for four people. He connects a signal generator to a loudspeaker. Each person being tested sits with their back to the loudspeaker and raises their hand every time they hear a sound from it.

(a) Briefly describe what Matthew should do to find the audible range of pitch for each person.

....

....

....

(b) Give **two** things that should be kept the same for each person to make sure that the results can be compared.

1 ....

2 ....

Matthew's results are shown opposite.

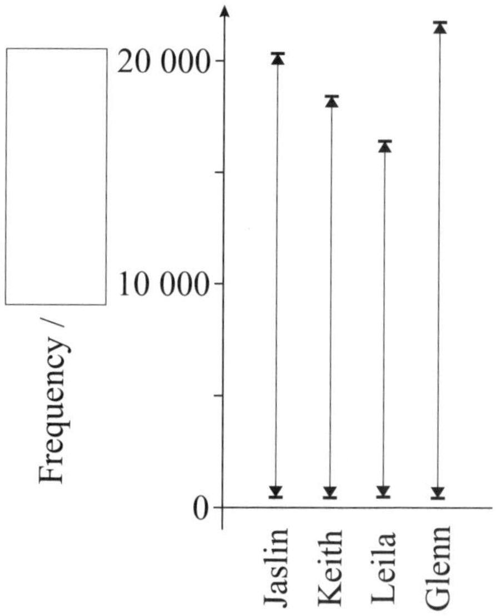

(c) Complete the graph by writing in the correct unit for frequency.

(d) Which person

(i) Has the largest audible range?

....

(ii) Is likely to be the oldest?

....

(iii) Is likely to be the youngest?

....

(e) Write down **two** possible causes of a smaller audible range of pitch, apart from age.

1 ....

2 ....

Light and Sound Mini-Exam

1 Tom's new clock has four different alarm sounds.
The patterns made by the sound waves on an oscilloscope screen are shown below.

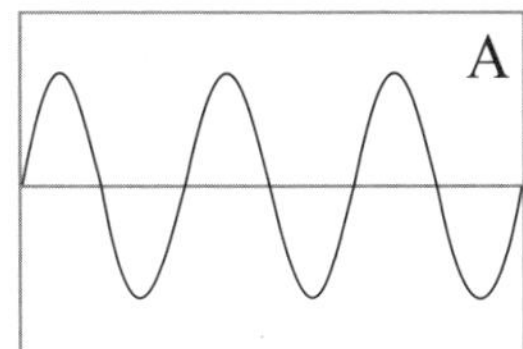

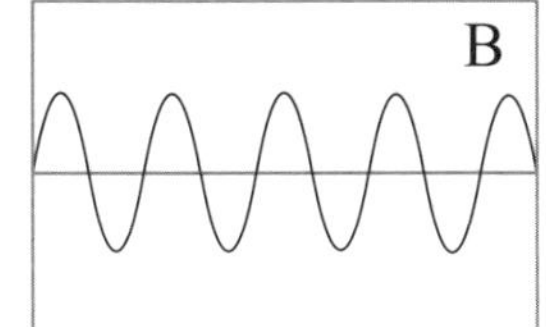

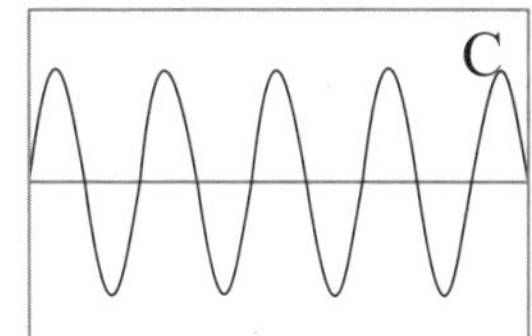

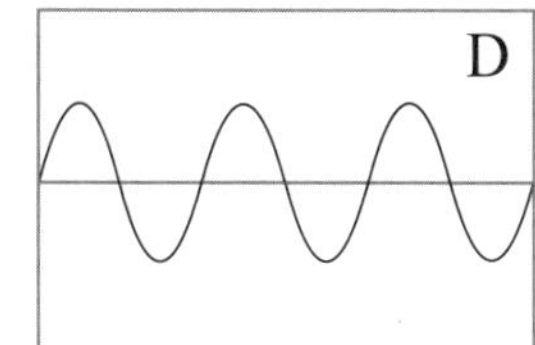

(a) Write the letters of the alarm sounds in the correct box in the table opposite.

	60 dB	80 dB
8000 Hz		
10 000 Hz		

(b) Which of the sound waves carry the same energy?

.... **and** ....

.... **and** ....

2 In one of the first experiments used to measure the speed of sound, a man called William Derham watched a cannon being fired 12 miles away. He started a timer when he saw the flash from the cannon, and stopped it when he heard the explosion.

(a) Explain why the time between seeing the flash and hearing the explosion was an accurate measure of the time the sound took to reach William Derham.

....

....

(b) William Derham found that changes in wind direction could change the time he recorded.

(i) Suggest why changes in wind direction could change the time it took William Derham to hear the explosion.

....

....

(ii) Suggest what he did to allow for this variation in his results.

....

....

Light and Sound Mini-Exam

3 **Lasers** produce very bright light.
A laser beam contains only one colour of light and travels in a very precise straight line.

The diagram below shows a laser beam shining onto glass.
Most of the light enters the glass, but some is reflected.

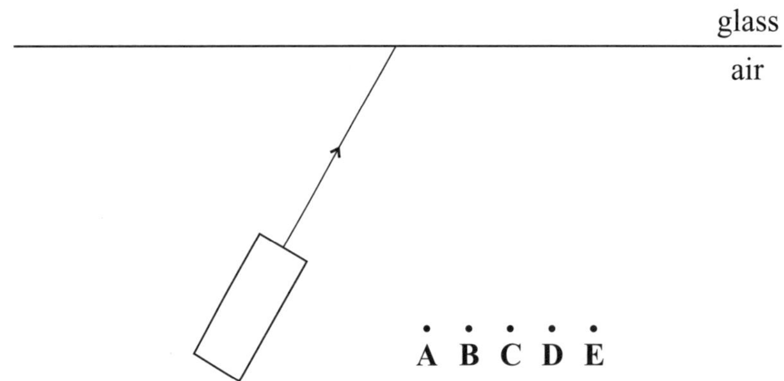

(a) What property of the glass means that light can travel through it?

....

(b) (i) What will happen to the light that enters the glass?

....

(ii) Explain why this happens.

....

....

....

(iii) Draw a ray of light on the diagram to show the path taken by the light that enters the glass.

(c) Which of the points **A** to **E** on the diagram will the **reflected** light pass through?
Explain how you know.

....

....

Light and Sound Mini-Exam

(d) Describe what will happen to the light if the glass is replaced with

(i) A mirror.

....

(ii) A sheet of white paper.

....

In the diagram below, a beam of green laser light travels through a glass prism and onto a white screen, where it appears as a spot of green light.

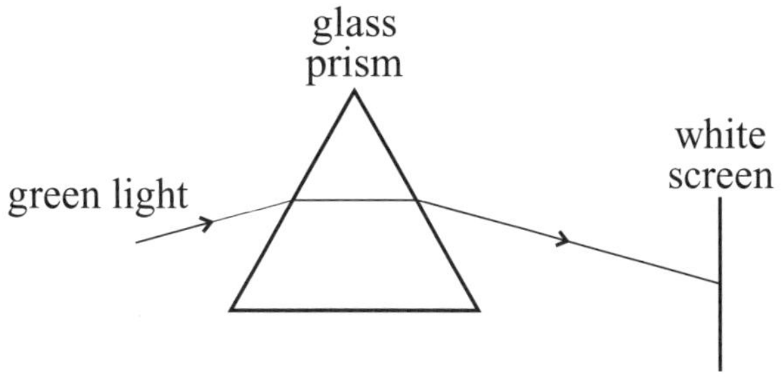

glass prism

white screen

green light

(e) (i) Describe what you would see if the screen was green. Explain your answer.

....

....

(ii) Describe what you would see if the screen was red. Explain your answer.

....

....

(f) The laser light is replaced with white light.

(i) What will appear on the screen? Explain why.

....

....

(ii) A blue filter is placed between the prism and the screen.
What will appear on the screen? Explain why.

....

....

Light and Sound Mini-Exam

4 A fishing boat is equipped with an **echo sounder** to help it find shoals of fish. The echo sounder sends pulses of high frequency sound into the ocean and detects any pulses that bounce back from objects underwater.

During one fishing trip, the boat sends out pulses of sound at three different locations. At the first two locations, the pulses come back after 3 s. At the third location, the pulse comes back after 1 s, then again after 3 s. The skipper decides to cast his nets at the third location.

(a) (i) Suggest what object causes the pulse to return to the boat after 3 s.

....

(ii) Explain the skipper's decision to cast his nets at the third location.

....

....

Below are three oscilloscope traces of pulses from the echo sounder.

A B C

(b) Which trace best represents the pulse

(i) When it is first sent out? ....

(ii) When it comes back after 1 s? ....

(iii) When it comes back after 3 s? ....

(c) Explain your answer to (b).

....

(d) The sound produced by the echo sounder has a large amplitude and a frequency well over 20 000 Hz. Explain why this is not a problem for fishermen, but some scientists are concerned about the effect on dolphins.

....

....

Day and Night

1 In the diagram opposite, Birmingham in England is labelled B, and Kuala Lumpur in Malaysia is labelled KL.

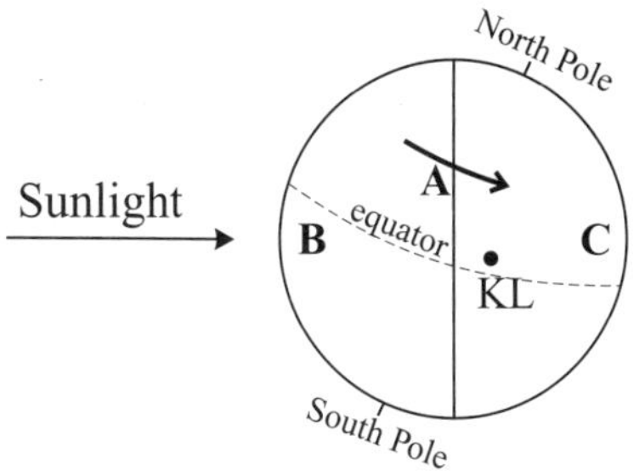

(a) Use the diagram to explain how day time changes to night time.

....

....

(b) Write **B** next to the statement that **best describes** the time of day in Birmingham, and **KL** next to the statement that **best describes** the time of day in Kuala Lumpur.

It is midday. .... The Sun has just set. ....

It is midnight. .... The Sun will rise soon. ....

2 The diagram shows the path of the Sun across the sky for one day in spring.

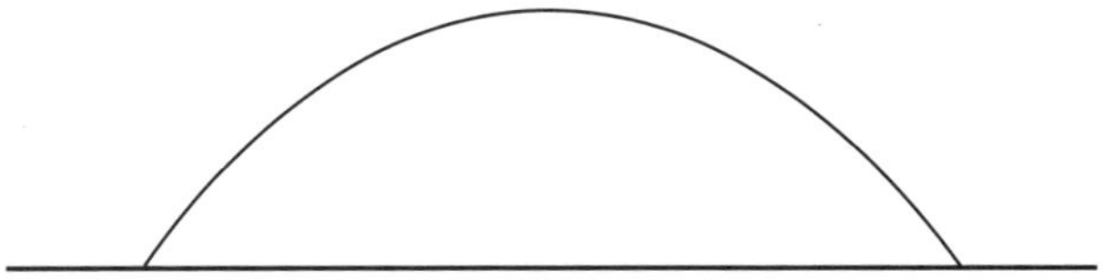

(a) (i) Mark the position of the Sun at midday with a cross.

(ii) Draw the path of the Sun across the sky for one day in winter. Label the path **winter**, and mark the position of the Sun at midday with a cross.

(iii) Draw the path of the Sun across the sky for one day in summer. Label the path **summer**, and mark the position of the Sun at midday with a cross.

(b) Are shadows at midday longest during **spring**, **summer** or **winter**? Explain your answer.

....

....

(c) Tick the **most accurate** of the following statements about the Sun.

It moves from east to west. ☐ It appears to move from west to east. ☐

It moves from west to east. ☐ It appears to move from east to west. ☐

Seasons

1 The diagrams below show the Earth at different times in a year.

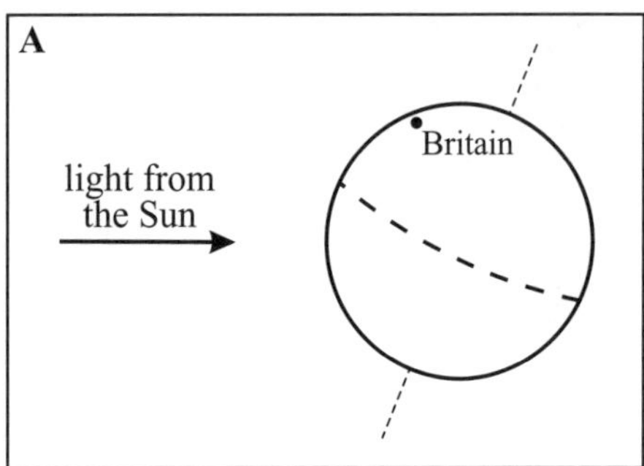

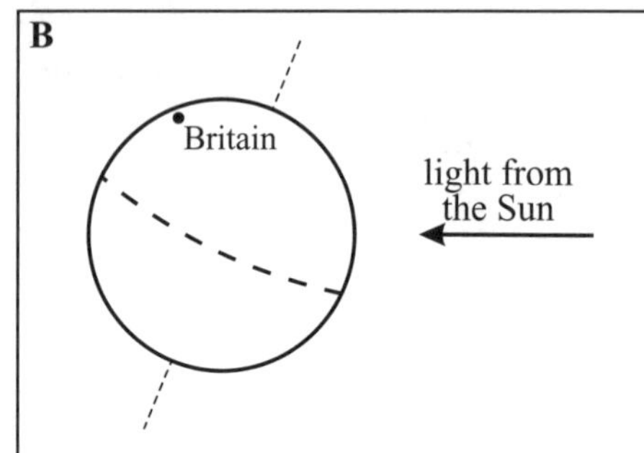

(a) (i) What is a year?

....

(ii) Explain why every fourth year is a leap year.

....

....

The Earth's tilt causes the seasons.

(b) Which diagram, **A** or **B,** shows Britain when it is

(i) summer? ....

(ii) winter? ....

(c) What **two** things are changed by the Earth's tilt, causing the seasons?

1 ....

2 ....

(d) Explain why it is summer in the southern hemisphere when it is winter in the northern hemisphere.

....

....

Satellites

1 The Earth has only one moon.

(a) Moons are natural satellites. Explain what is meant by this statement.

....

....

(b) Even though it has no light of its own, the Moon is usually the brightest object in the night sky. Explain why.

....

The diagram below shows the Moon at different points in its orbit.

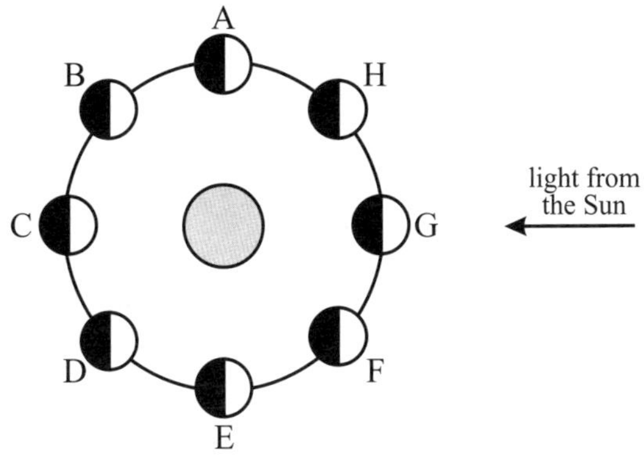

(c) Explain why the Moon appears to change shape as it orbits the Earth.

....

....

(d) Use the information below to answer the questions that follow.

When the whole face of the Moon can be seen, it is called a **Full** Moon.
When the face of the Moon is more than half but less than fully visible, it is called a **gibbous** Moon.
When the face of the Moon is less than half visible, it is called a **crescent** Moon.
When the Moon cannot be seen at all, it is called a **New** Moon.

At which of the points **A** to **H** in the diagram above will the Moon be

(i) Full? ....

(ii) Gibbous? ....

(iii) Crescent? ....

(iv) New? ....

Gravity

1 The diagrams on the right show Jupiter and one of its forty-seven known moons, and the Earth and its only moon.

(a) (i) What is the name of the force that keeps the moons in orbit around the planets?

....

(ii) Draw an arrow on each of the diagrams to show the direction of the force that keeps the moons in orbit around the planets.

(b) Io and the Moon have about the same mass, but Jupiter has a **much** larger mass than the Earth. Will the force that keeps Io in orbit be **larger** than, **the same** as or **smaller** than the force that keeps the Moon in orbit around the Earth? Explain your answer.

....

....

(c) The Moon's orbit is circular. Suggest why Jupiter's moons **don't** tend to have circular orbits.

....

2 The diagram shows a satellite orbiting a planet. It has released a probe.

(a) The force of gravity between the planet and the satellite keeps the satellite in orbit. What happened to the size of this force after the probe was released? Explain your answer.

....

....

(b) A force of gravity between the planet and the probe is pulling the probe down towards the surface. What will happen to the size of this force as the probe gets nearer to the surface? Explain your answer.

....

....

Artificial Satellites

1 The diagram below shows a communications satellite.
Stations on the ground transmit and receive signals from the satellite.

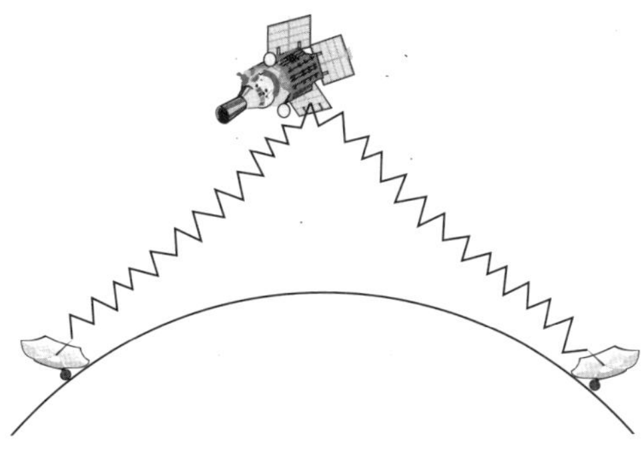

(a) Using the diagram, suggest why a signal is not sent directly between stations.

....

....

(b) The satellite is **geostationary**. It stays above the same place on the Earth's surface, even though it is orbiting the Earth continually.

(i) Suggest how the satellite stays above the same place on the Earth's surface.

....

....

(ii) How long will the satellite take to complete one orbit?

....

(c) Describe **three** other uses of artificial satellites, apart from communications.

1 ....

....

2 ....

....

3 ....

....

The Solar System

1 All the planets in the Solar System are visible from Earth. Mercury is between the Earth and the Sun. Venus is the brightest object in the sky apart from the Sun and the Moon, but Mercury is the most difficult to see.

(a) What is a planet?

....

(b) Explain why the planets in the Solar System are visible from Earth, even though they don't give out light.

....

(c) Suggest **one** reason for Venus's brightness.

....

(d) Suggest why Mercury is the most difficult planet to see.

....

2 Below is a simplified diagram of the orbits of Venus, Earth, Mars and Jupiter, and a table showing their orbit times to the nearest half year.

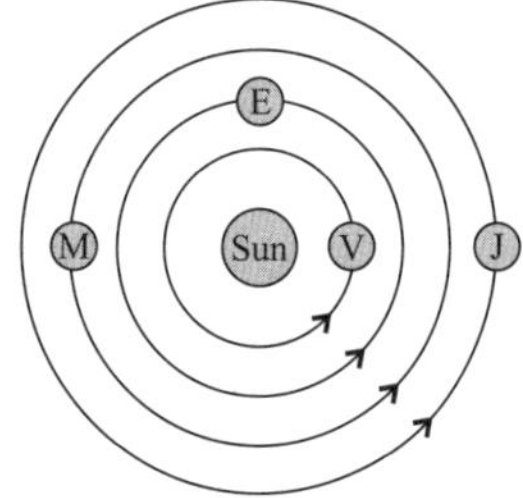

Planet	Orbit time (Earth years)
Venus	0.5
Earth	1.0
Mars	2.0
Jupiter	12.0

(a) On the diagram, mark the approximate position of each planet in six Earth months' time with a cross.

(b) Describe the relationship between a planet's distance from the Sun and its orbit time.

....

(c) Give **one** way in which the orbits shown in the diagram are simplified.

....

The Solar System

1 The table on the right contains information about the **planets** in our Solar System.

Planet	Relative size	Relative mass
Earth	1.0	1.0
Jupiter	11.0	318.0
Mars	0.5	0.1
Mercury	0.4	0.05
Neptune	3.8	17.0
Pluto	0.2	0.003
Saturn	9.4	95.0
Uranus	4.0	15.0
Venus	0.9	0.8

(a) What is meant by the word **relative** in the table?

....

....

....

....

(b) In both **size** and **mass**, which of the planets is

(i) largest? ....

(ii) smallest? ....

(iii) most like Earth? ....

(c) (i) Which planet is the third largest in **size**?

....

(ii) Which planet is the third largest in **mass**?

....

(iii) Explain the difference between the **size** and the **mass** of a planet.

....

....

(d) Explain why the Sun is not included in the table.

....

....

(e) Name **two** other objects in the Solar System that do not appear in the table.

1 .... 2 ....

Beyond the Solar System

1 It was not until last century that astronomers began to discover galaxies other than ours. Planets outside our Solar System have been found only in the last few years.

(a) Write down the following objects in order of size, smallest first.

the Sun **Solar System** **Universe** **planet Earth** **galaxy**

.... **smallest**

....

....

....

.... **largest**

(b) (i) What is a galaxy?

....

(ii) What name is given to our own galaxy?

....

(iii) Describe what a galaxy other than our own looks like from Earth.

....

(c) Suggest **two** reasons why planets orbiting stars other than the Sun were not discovered until recently.

1 ....

....

2 ....

....

The Earth and Beyond Mini-Exam

1 Sanjay took a photo at night by leaving the shutter of his camera open for about a few hours.
The diagram on the right shows the picture he got.

(a) What causes the stars in Sanjay's photo to look like they are spinning around the night sky?

....

(b) One star in the photo doesn't seem to move.

(i) What is this star called?

....

(ii) Why doesn't the star appear to move?

....

2 The diagram on the right shows two artificial satellites in orbit around the Earth. One satellite orbits round the poles and the other orbits round the equator.

A

B

(a) One satellite has an orbit of 2 hours, and the other 24 hours.
If both satellites are travelling at the same speed, which satellite is more likely to take 24 hours to complete an orbit — **A** or **B**? Explain your answer.

....

....

(b) One satellite monitors the weather and the other relays a TV signal.
Suggest which is which? Give a reason for your answers.

Satellite .... **is likely to be the weather satellite because** ....

....

Satellite .... **is likely to be the television satellite because** ....

....

The Earth and Beyond Mini-Exam

3 The position of Earth at various points in its orbit around the Sun is shown in the diagram below. Some of the stars in the constellation Orion are also shown. Note that the diagram is not to scale — Orion is **very** far from our Solar System.

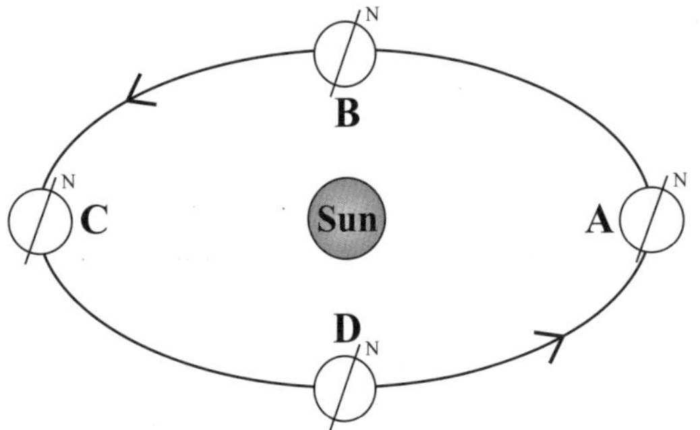

Orion

(a) How long does the Earth take to complete one orbit, in days?
Answer as accurately as you can.

....

(b) (i) What is the Sun?

....

(ii) Describe **two** effects the Sun has on planet Earth.

1 ....

2 ....

(c) The height the Sun reaches in Earth's sky changes depending on the position of the Earth in its orbit.

(i) What causes the Sun to 'move' across Earth's sky once every 24 hours?

....

....

(ii) At which point in the Earth's orbit will the Sun appear lowest in the sky in the Northern hemisphere at midday — **A**, **B**, **C** or **D**? ....

The Earth and Beyond Mini-Exam

(iii) Explain your answer to (ii), using the diagram below to help.

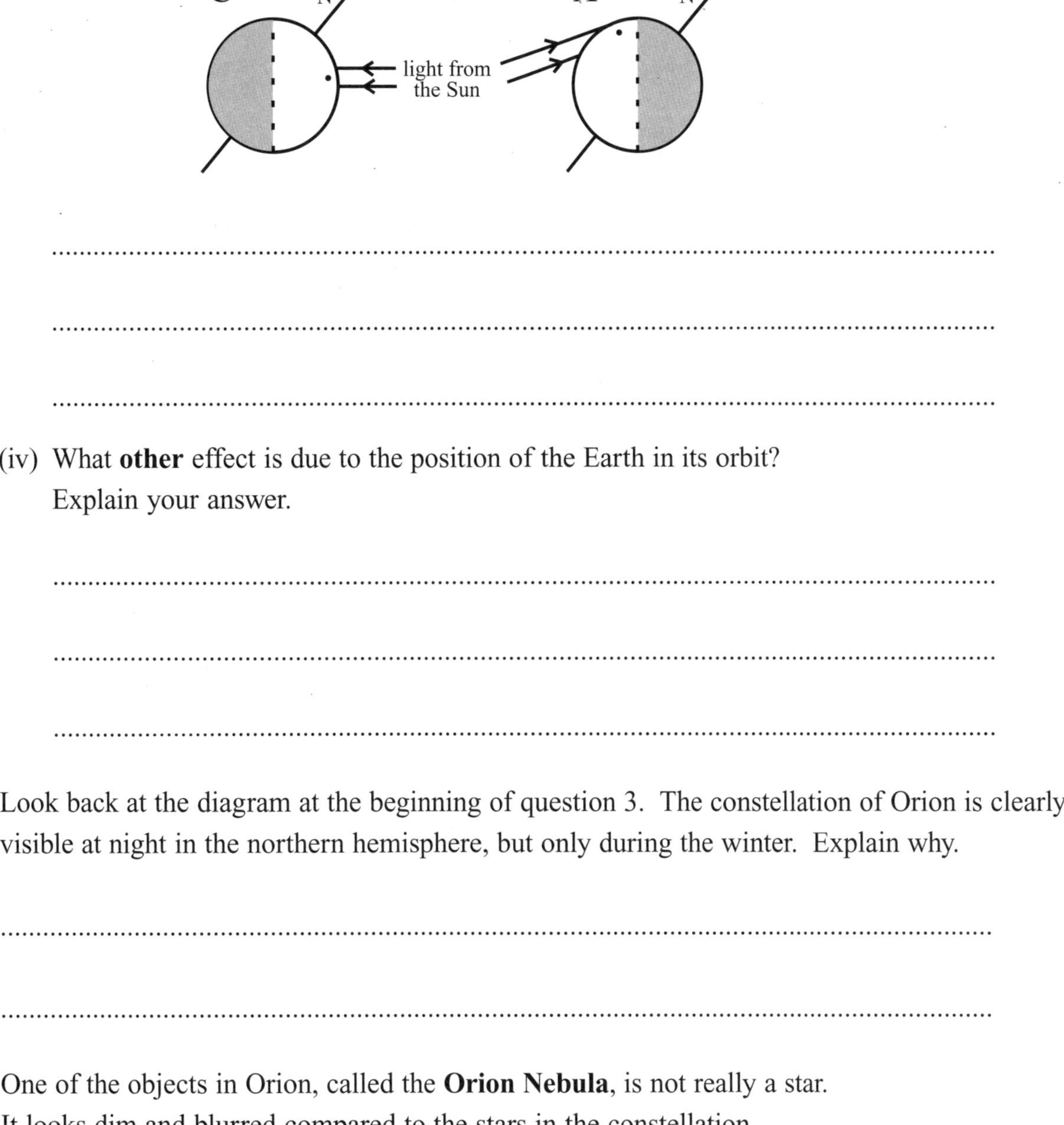

....

....

....

(iv) What **other** effect is due to the position of the Earth in its orbit?
Explain your answer.

....

....

....

(d) Look back at the diagram at the beginning of question 3. The constellation of Orion is clearly visible at night in the northern hemisphere, but only during the winter. Explain why.

....

....

(e) One of the objects in Orion, called the **Orion Nebula**, is not really a star.
It looks dim and blurred compared to the stars in the constellation.
Suggest what the Orion Nebula might be. Explain your answer.

....

....

The Earth and Beyond Mini-Exam

4 The Solar System is held together by the gravity of the Sun.

(a) What is gravity?

....

(b) Explain why it is the gravity of the Sun that holds the Solar System together.

....

....

(c) Comets are giant, frozen masses that travel right to the edges of the Solar System. The diagram on the right shows the orbit of one comet around the Sun.

(i) What term is used to describe the **shape** of the comet's orbit?

....

(ii) The comet is much smaller than any of the planets in the Solar System. Suggest why its orbit is much larger.

....

....

(iii) What will happen to the gravity affecting the comet as it gets closer to the Sun? Explain your answer.

....

....

(d) The Earth's orbit gives it just the right amount of heat from the Sun to sustain life.

(i) Suggest which **two** planets orbit just outside this area.

1 .... 2 ....

(ii) Suggest why life cannot be sustained on these two planets.

Planet 1 ....

Planet 2 ....

Forms of Energy

1 Different forms of energy are needed for different activities.

(a) Write down the **main** form of energy being demonstrated in each of the diagrams below.

(i) ....

(iii) ....

(ii) Supercell ....

(iv) ....

(b) Draw lines to join each form of energy on the left to the **most appropriate** example on the right.

chemical	**digging the garden**
sound	**the energy flowing from a power station**
gravitational potential	**a bar of chocolate**
kinetic	**loud music on the radio**
electrical	**a skydiver stepping out of an aeroplane**

2 Jimmy is sitting by a fire to keep warm.

(a) He says that there's no heat in his body. Is he right? Explain your answer.

....

....

(b) He says that the temperature of the fire is flowing into his body.
Is he right? Explain your answer.

....

....

Energy Transformations

1 An electric toothbrush has a rechargeable battery.

(a) Tick the correct box to show the energy transformation taking place as the battery is recharged.

☐ kinetic to sound ☐ electrical to chemical

☐ chemical to electrical ☐ heat to kinetic

(b) What **useful** energy transformation takes place when the brush is used? Tick the correct box.

☐ electrical to kinetic to sound ☐ electrical to chemical to kinetic

☐ chemical to electrical to kinetic ☐ chemical to sound to kinetic

2 Write down the energy transformations happening in the pictures below. (Note that **one** form of energy can be transferred to become **more than one** form.)

(a)

....

(b)

....

(c)

....

(d)

....

Transfer of Energy

1 Oliver heats one end of a piece of copper wire in a Bunsen burner flame.
The other end of the wire soon gets hot as well.

(a) Why is heat energy transferred along the wire?

....

(b) What process transfers the heat energy along the wire?

....

(c) Describe how the heat energy is transferred along the wire.

....

....

....

2 Gliders make use of rising currents of warm air called **thermals**.

(a) Name the process by which thermals transfer heat energy.

....

(b) Why are there no thermals in a vacuum such as outer space?

....

....

3 Tankers visit farms every day to collect milk. The milk must be kept cold to help it stay fresh.

(a) Describe how the heat of the Sun could be transferred to the milk inside the tankers.

....

....

(b) Suggest why milk tankers are usually a shiny silver colour.

....

....

Energy Resources

1 **Light** from the Sun provides us with energy resources in the form of **fossil fuels** and **biomass**.

(a) Explain why plants are important in the production of these energy resources.

....

....

(b) Describe how fossil fuels are formed.

....

....

....

(c) Name **two** types of biomass we use as energy resources.

1 .... 2 ....

(d) For **one** of the energy resources named in (c), describe the chain of energy transformations that converts the light energy from the Sun into a form that we use.

....

....

2 Winds are an energy resource. Wind turbines can be used to generate electricity.

(a) (i) What form of energy is the energy of wind?

....

(ii) Using the diagram below, explain how the energy of the Sun causes winds.

....

....

....

....

(b) What other energy resource results from winds?

....

Generating Electricity

1 Our electricity is generated in power stations.

(a) Name **three** fuels that are burnt in power stations.

1 .... 2 .... 3 ....

(b) Explain why petrol is **not** burnt in power stations.

....

(c) Give **two** important uses of electricity within the home.

1 .... 2 ....

2 The three main parts of a power station are shown below.

A B C

(a) Write down the **letters** of the parts in the order that they are used to generate electricity. Write the **name** of the part next to each letter.

1 **Letter** .... **Name** ....

2 **Letter** .... **Name** ....

3 **Letter** .... **Name** ....

(b) Describe how the parts convert the chemical energy in fuels into electrical energy we can use in our homes.

....

....

....

....

....

Generating Electricity

1 The amount of fossil fuels burnt can be reduced by **saving energy** and by using **renewable energy resources** instead.

(a) Explain why scientists warn that we should reduce the rate at which we are burning fossil fuels.

....

....

(b) Suggest **two** ways of saving energy.

1 ....

2 ....

(c) (i) Name **three** renewable energy resources that could be used to replace fossil fuels.

1 ....

2 ....

3 ....

(ii) Explain why these resources are called **renewable** rather than **re-usable**.

....

....

2 Many calculators have a solar cell like the one in the picture.

(a) What energy transformation takes place in the calculator?

.... ⟶ ....

(b) Write down **two** advantages of using a solar cell in a calculator.

1 ....

2 ....

(c) Give **one** disadvantage.

....

Conservation of Energy

1 Answer the following questions about energy.

(a) Gemma says that heat energy can be created by rubbing two sticks together really fast. Is she correct? Explain your answer.

....

....

(b) Put a tick in the boxes next to the statements that are **true** below.

- [ ] **Energy is only useful when it's converted from one form into another.**
- [ ] **Output energy from machines is the same as input energy, but more useful.**
- [ ] **Energy is always useful.**
- [ ] **Machines convert input energy into useful output energy.**

(c) Gemma notices that the computer room at school is warmer and noisier than the other classrooms. Explain why this might be, in terms of energy.

....

....

2 For each machine below, name the form of the energy input, the useful form of energy output and the form in which energy is wasted. (Note that more than one form of energy may be used or wasted.)

(a)

Energy input ....

Useful energy output ....

Wasted energy output ....

(b)

Energy input ....

Useful energy output ....

Wasted energy output ....

Conservation of Energy

1 Look at the pictures of the two light bulbs.
The ordinary light bulb has an energy input of 100 joules per second.
The energy saver light bulb has an energy input of 20 joules per second.
Both bulbs give out the same amount of light energy per second.

100W — ordinary light bulb

20W — energy saver light bulb

(a) Explain how it is possible that both bulbs can give out the same amount of light energy per second.

....

(b) Suggest **two** advantages of using the energy saver bulbs instead of the ordinary bulbs.

1 ....

2 ....

2 A petrol-engined car, electric lawnmower and wind turbine all waste energy at different rates.

(a) Calculate the following energy values for each device.

(i) For every 100 joules of energy input, the car wastes 75 joules.

Useful energy = ... **joules**

(ii) For every 80 joules of useful energy output, the lawnmower wastes 120 joules.

Input energy = ... **joules**

(iii) The wind turbine has an energy input of 400 joules and an energy output of 80 joules.

Wasted energy = ... **joules**

(b) What is the **useful** form of energy output by:

(i) both the car and the lawnmower? ....

(ii) the wind turbine? ....

(c) Which device is

(i) **most** wasteful of energy? ....

(ii) **least** wasteful of energy? ....

(d) Name **two** forms of energy wasted by all three devices.

1 .... 2 ....

Energy Resources and Energy Mini-Exam

1 The diagram on the right shows a design for an oven.

steel shell
OUTSIDE OF OVEN
INSIDE OF OVEN
aluminium foil sheet
polystyrene

(a) Steel is a good heat conductor.
Describe how heat energy is transferred through steel.

....

....

(b) Polystyrene is **not** a good heat conductor. Suggest why it is used in the oven.

....

....

(c) Aluminium foil is shiny and smooth. Suggest why it is used in the oven.

....

2 The picture shows the inside of an electric kettle.

water
element

(a) What energy transformation takes place in the **element** when the kettle is switched on?

....

(b) (i) The water in the kettle already has some energy. Explain this statement.

....

(ii) Explain why the water gains more energy from the element.

....

(c) (i) Name the process by which energy is transferred through the water.

....

(ii) Explain why the element is placed at the **bottom** of the kettle.
Use the word 'convection' in your answer.

....

....

Energy Resources and Energy Mini-Exam

3 Agnes is using a food mixer to make cake mix.

(a) The useful energy output of the food mixer is less than the electrical energy input. Agnes states that "some of the energy disappears."

(i) Explain why Agnes's statement is incorrect.

....

....

(ii) The diagram below shows the energy transformations that happen in the food mixer. Fill in the missing information.

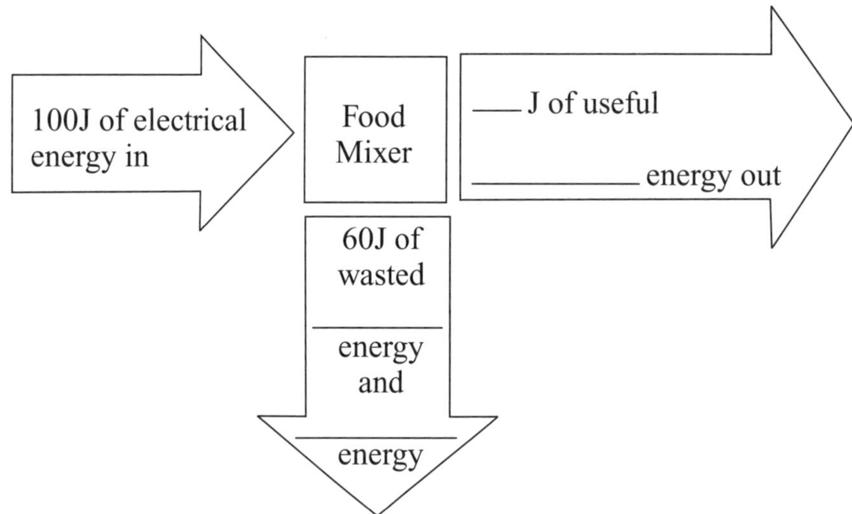

(b) The electricity grid that the food mixer is connected to is supplied by a **coal-fired** power station and a **hydroelectric** power station.

A simplified diagram of the hydroelectric power station is shown below. As the water flows downhill, it spins a turbine. The turbine is connected to a generator.

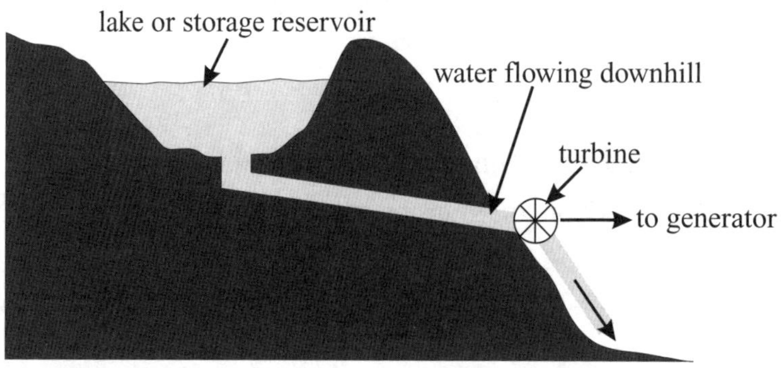

Energy Resources and Energy Mini-Exam

Fill in the gaps in the following sentences to show the **useful** energy transformations that take place at the hydroelectric power station.

The .... energy of the water is

converted to .... energy as

the water flows downhill.

The .... energy is converted to

.. energy in the generator.

(c) The electrical energy generated in both the coal-fired power station and the hydroelectric power station originally comes from the Sun.

(i) Explain how the Sun provides the energy in the coal burnt in the coal-fired power station.

....

....

(ii) Suggest how the Sun provides the energy that is converted into electrical energy in the hydroelectric power station.

....

(d) The turbines used in both power stations waste some energy.

(i) Name **one** form of energy wasted in a turbine.

....

(ii) Reducing the energy wasted in the turbines is one way of saving our energy resources. Explain why this is particularly important in the coal-fired power station.

....

....

....

Energy Resources and Energy Mini-Exam

4 John is loading a lorry with large stone blocks from a pile on the ground.

(a) As he lifts a block, energy is transferred from John to the block.

(i) What form is the energy in before John lifts the block?

....

(ii) Where is the energy stored before John lifts the block?

....

(b) (i) As John lifts a block off the ground and up to the height of the lorry, the block has energy in **two** different forms. What are they?

1 ....

2 ....

(ii) The energy is stored in the block when it is on the back of the lorry. What form is the energy in?

....

(c) One of the blocks is placed badly on the lorry, and falls off.

(i) What energy transformation takes place as the block falls?

....

(ii) What energy transformation takes place when the block hits the ground?

....